Tending Body, Heart, Mind & Soul

Tending Body, Heart, Mind & Soul

Following Jesus in Caring for Ourselves

Mary Jane Gorman

ABINGDON PRESS
Nashville

TENDING BODY, HEART, MIND, AND SOUL
FOLLOWING JESUS IN CARING FOR OURSELVES

Copyright © 2006 by Mary Jane Gorman

This book is printed on acid-free paper.

Library of Congress Cataloging-in-Publication Data

Gorman, Mary Jane, 1983-
   Tending body, heart, mind, and soul : following Jesus in caring for ourselves / Mary Jane Gorman.
      p. cm.
   ISBN 0-687-49210-6 (pbk. : alk. paper)
   1. Jesus Christ—Humanity—Biblical teaching. 2. Bible. N.T. Gospels—Criticism, interpretation, etc. 3. Body, Human—Religious aspects—Christianity. 4. Caring—Religious aspects—Christianity. I. Title.

   BT218.G67 2006
   248.4—dc22

                                                          2006017129

Scripture quotations unless noted otherwise are taken from the *New Revised Standard Version of the Bible*, copyright 1989, by the Division of Christian Education of the National Council of the Churches of Christ in the United States of America. Used by permission. All rights reserved.

Scripture noted KJV is from the King James or Authorized Version of the Bible.

06 07 08 09 10 11 12 13 14 15—10 9 8 7 6 5 4 3 2 1
MANUFACTURED IN THE UNITED STATES OF AMERICA

Contents

1. Schedule
2.

Introduction

HOW DO YOU RESPOND WHEN ASKED TO DESCRIBE A PERSON YOU KNOW well? If someone said, "Tell me about your best friend (or your next door neighbor or your business partner or your sister)," what characteristics would you choose to mention? Would you describe your friend's high level of energy or quick wit or positive attitude? Would you say how smart or attractive or generous she or he is? Suppose the person said instead, "Tell me about Jesus." Would you answer in an entirely different way, talking about what you believe about who Jesus was or who he is in your life?

Now suppose you were asked to write a letter of recommendation for Jesus to a social service agency looking for a volunteer counselor or to a personnel director hiring an upper-level manager. What would you say? Have you thought about what kind of man Jesus was? Have you ever considered his habits, intellect, and personality?

When we focus solely on Jesus' teaching and preaching, we may not notice descriptions about the man himself. In being attentive only to what we believe about Jesus, we may neglect insight into how he lived and who he was.

If we are to follow Jesus, we must look more closely and personally at the man we are following—not only at how he told us to live, but also at how he, himself, chose to live. This book calls you to look closely at Jesus, to be attentive to his humanity. The reflections focus on how Jesus took care of his entire being: body, heart, mind, and soul. The insights shared are based on gospel texts—often on the verses other than those containing the "major" teachings, parables, and encounters. At times, you will be invited to read between the lines of the gospel texts and to speculate about Jesus' thoughts, expressions, or feelings.

~ *Introduction* ~

The verb used throughout the book to describe Jesus' self-care is
tending. If this seems a strange choice of words, consider the kinds of
things we tend. We speak of tending a garden. Among other activities,
we plant, weed, fertilize, and water the garden. We take care of, tend,
the garden. Or, we may tend a sick child or an elderly parent by assist-
ing with practical needs such as feeding or bathing or giving medica-
tion. We take care of, tend, the person needing our help. Similarly, in
John 21:16, Jesus tells Peter, "Tend my sheep." Jesus did not mean this
literally. Rather, Jesus wanted Peter and the other disciples to offer care
and attention—to show love—for all the children of God. Tending,
then, is an act of caring. It reflects a commitment to meet the needs of
something or someone. The word suggests more than a dutiful act; it is
extending tender attention.

The gospel narratives suggest that Jesus tended others as well as
himself in four ways: physically, emotionally, mentally, and spiritually.
In the Scriptures we find evidence of his careful attention to his own
body, heart, mind, and soul. In fact, tending one's own self may be a
necessary condition for obeying what Jesus called the greatest commandment: "Hear, O Israel: the Lord our God, the Lord is one; you
shall love the Lord your God with all your heart, and with all your soul,
and with all your mind, and with all your strength" (Mark 12:29-30).
The commandment calls us to love God with our whole being, which is
composed of different dimensions. Each part of who we are—body,
heart, mind, and soul—must be given careful attention if we are to
be fit for the task of loving God. The same holds true for loving our
neighbor, which Jesus said is the second commandment (Mark 12:31).
Jesus is our model, showing us how we can tend ourselves. While this
tending is a loving act, it is not an end in itself. Our tending makes us
available and prepared to love God and neighbor as we are commanded
to do.

As you make your way through the chapters of this book, you will
consider some specific ways that Jesus tended the four aspects of his
being: body, heart, mind, and soul. Following an overview of each
topic, a reflection on a specific gospel passage will move you to a closer, deeper look at how Jesus tended this particular aspect of his being.

The topics addressed in each section have been chosen based on sufficient and compelling evidence that Jesus did, in fact, tend his body,

heart, mind, or soul in the ways described. For example, numerous accounts in the Gospels reveal how Jesus tended his heart by the way that he dealt with his grief. Certainly there are other ways of tending the heart; by no means does this book provide an exhaustive list of ways to tend any of the aspects of our being. In fact, after considering a particular aspect of Jesus' self-tending, you may become engaged in trying to find additional examples yourself.

The book closes with a discussion of the interconnection of body, heart, mind, and soul, illustrating that Jesus' tending of himself was, ultimately, a tending toward wholeness. Jesus is our model of what it means to be whole.

Although this is not a self-help book intended to document specific instruction, such as how Jesus wants you to exercise your body or express your anger, it will help you to look carefully at the behavior, habits, and personality of Jesus and consider personal application for your own life. Questions for reflection and discussion are provided for each section, making the material ideal for both personal and group study.

I invite you to draw closer to the man Jesus—to recognize and reflect on who he was and what he did. In doing so, you will be prompted to reflect on your own path toward wholeness.

1. Tending the Body

ALMOST DAILY WE ARE BOMBARDED WITH THE LATEST SCIENTIFIC warnings and medical advice telling us how to be healthy. We get extensive, and often conflicting, information from newspapers, television and magazines. Likewise, the Internet gives us access to an almost endless supply of medical facts and advice. In these and other sources, attention to physical health is generally separate from attention to spiritual health, although increasingly the subjects are overlapping. The regional hospital may house a center for spiritual healing, and the local church may sponsor a weight-reduction support group. Does concern and care for the body, however, have any connection to Jesus, to what we know about him and what we can learn from him?

How did Jesus tend his body? Perhaps a prior question is this: Did Jesus, either intentionally or unintentionally, take care of his body at all? Our recollection of Jesus making reference to his body may focus on the supper when he said, "This is my body" (Luke 22:19). Or, we may hear the phrase "Jesus' body" and associate it with what Joseph of Arimathea received and wrapped in a linen cloth (Matthew 27:57-59). Jesus' words elsewhere in the Gospels may cause us to think, rightly or wrongly, of the body as the source of sinful behavior (Matthew 5:29) or as a less important part of our being (Matthew 10:28). These words and others may cause us to separate "religious" notions of the body from contemporary concerns about physical health.

Although Jesus' words more often centered on the heart, mind, and soul, certainly his sacramental words and words of warning about the body are not to be ignored. Did he, however, neglect entirely the health and well-being of the body, the most "earthy" aspect of our being? If we think that the Gospels turn our attention only toward heaven and eternal life, we may ignore the body, or at least separate it from our religious and spiritual concerns. Before doing that, let us look again at Jesus.

Jesus did not ignore the bodies of those with whom and to whom he ministered. Quite the contrary, his healing ministry reveals clearly that he was concerned about the bodies of other people. He did not tell others to accept their physical suffering and to concern themselves only with seeking forgiveness and the promise of a better life in heaven. No, Jesus healed the lame, the blind, and the leper. He healed those with bleeding and those with epilepsy. The health of the body mattered to Jesus.

Consider Jesus and his own body. Did he ignore his own physical well-being? Was he a burn-the-candle-at-both-ends kind of guy to whom his disciples each dared the other to say, "Physician, heal thyself"? Was he an overweight, short of breath, slow-moving man who constantly frustrated his disciples because of his lack of energy and stamina? No, Jesus was neither of these types. In fact, Jesus did tend his body with the *food* he ate, with the *exercise* that was part of his daily life, with the *rest* he insisted on receiving, and with *touch*—the physical touch of one person with another. We, too, can tend our bodies in each of these ways.

Food

Walk into any major bookstore and go to the health and diet books section. There you will find shelf after shelf of books devoted to what we should eat to receive various health benefits, such as achieving a healthy weight, preventing disease, and maintaining a youthful appearance. Add to this collection of books the multiple shelves of cookbooks, and one might conclude that our culture is obsessed with food and eating. After perusing these books more closely or doing a quick Internet search, you would notice numerous food and diet books based on or referring to biblical texts. Should we look to Jesus for guidance about what we should eat? Do we know enough about the diet Jesus ate to use it as a model for our own menus?

During his ministry, Jesus often was invited to dine in the homes of followers. Was he regularly served a rich meal of meat, cheese, and wine by well-to-do hosts trying to impress the popular teacher with an unusually extravagant feast? Did he more often share a meager meal with a poor household of followers? Certainly Jesus ate the food available to him in the Mediterranean region in which he lived. We could look for further clues to his diet by studying, for example, Jewish dietary laws and the foods mentioned in the Gospels. Suppose we gather enough information to produce a typical weekly menu for Jesus. Should we eat this "Jesus diet" because that is what Jesus ate? Well, perhaps not. Can we conclude anything about how Jesus tended his body with the food he ate? If so, should we develop a model for our own eating habits from his example?

We read in the Gospels that Jesus attended feasts, banquets, and dinners given in his honor and that critics accused him of being a glutton and a drunkard. Certainly Jesus could have cultivated a group of followers with the means to feed him lavishly on a regular basis. Most of what we find in the Gospels, however, suggests that Jesus usually dined simply. That Jesus considered bread and fish an adequate meal is indicated by his offering this simple meal to thousands of people on two separate occasions (Mark 6:35-44; 8:1-9). Likewise, after his resurrection, Jesus is reported to have shared this simple meal of bread and fish with his disciples (John 21:9-14). The provisions carried by Jesus and his disciples on a journey also suggest the simplicity of their regular diet. After boarding a boat and starting across the sea, the disciples realized that they "had forgotten to bring any bread; and they had only one loaf with them in the boat" (Mark 8:14).

All that we read indicates that Jesus was vigorous. While some people do eat unhealthy food and stay vigorous (at least to the age of Jesus during his ministry), we can reasonably speculate that Jesus' physical energy was due in part to his simple, healthy diet. We should be attentive to this example of Jesus' lifestyle. However, looking solely to the Gospels to determine our diets would be challenging and might cause us to miss some important points that Jesus makes about food that are not about the supper menu.

The religious leaders of the day focused on fasting, on ritual washing before eating, and on foods that should not be eaten at all because they were "unclean." Although Jesus fasted for forty days in the wilderness before beginning his ministry and talked about one's appearance when one fasted, Jesus and his disciples were said to be unlike John the

Baptist and his disciples who did fast. Furthermore, the Pharisees accused the disciples of not washing their hands properly and of not following all the Jewish dietary laws. Jesus said, "There is nothing outside a person that by going in can defile, but the things that come out are what defile" (Mark 7:15). In denying that food could "defile" a person, Jesus was not addressing issues of fatty foods being bad for the heart or tainted food being bad for the stomach. Jesus was saying that eating or refraining from eating, the method of washing before eating, and the particular foods eaten are not what matter most to God.

Unlike the Pharisees, Jesus' attitude about food and the need to eat was practical. When thousands of people were hungry after listening to Jesus preach for several days, Jesus fed them a simple meal of bread and fish. When describing those who would inherit the kingdom, Jesus began with "for I was hungry and you gave me food" (Matthew 25:35). When people are hungry, they need food to eat. Jesus never denied that the body needs to be tended with adequate food.

Although Jesus affirmed basic needs, his attitude toward food might be described as carefree. Perhaps the best description of this attitude is found in these words from the Sermon on the Mount: "Therefore I tell you, do not worry about your life, what you will eat. . . . Is not life more than food . . . ?" (Matthew 6:25). Surely Jesus did not mean that people in drought-ridden or war-torn regions should have no concern that they and their children are starving. We are to be responsible and to do whatever we can to take care of ourselves, those dependent on us, and others who cannot provide for themselves. The message here is that we are not to worry about providing. We may think that we are not anxious about food. We have all we want and need—and often much more than we need. Perhaps, however, we do worry about whether the food is low-fat enough for our diet, or elegant enough for the dinner party, or fast enough to prepare for the children who soon have to be at some activity elsewhere. Jesus seemed to be saying that we are not to worry about food in these or any other ways. He also implied that we are to share food with our neighbors in need so that they will not worry, either.

How did Jesus tend his body? Think about a loaf of bread. It is simple, healthy food. It can satisfy our hunger. It is something to share with others who are hungry but have no bread. We should not worry about our bread because it alone cannot give us life. Look at the bread and remember Jesus. As we continue to look at Jesus, we will see that eating the bread and following the Bread of Life are nourishing and satisfying for the body, heart, mind, and soul.

"Make Them Sit Down"

The day was drawing to a close, and the twelve came to him and said, "Send the crowd away, so that they may go into the surrounding villages and countryside, to lodge and get provisions; for we are here in a deserted place." But he said to them, "You give them something to eat." They said, "We have no more than five loaves and two fish—unless we are to go and buy food for all these people." For there were about five thousand men. And he said to his disciples, "Make them sit down in groups of about fifty each." They did so and made them all sit down. And taking the five loaves and the two fish, he looked up to heaven, and blessed and broke them, and gave them to the disciples to set before the crowd. And all ate and were filled. What was left over was gathered up, twelve baskets of broken pieces. (Luke 9:12-17)

In this familiar story, the disciples come to Jesus to focus his attention on practical matters. Late in the day, the people who have been listening to Jesus are tired and hungry. Perhaps the disciples are the ones who are particularly tired and hungry. They may be eager for the crowd to leave so that they can fix supper! Jesus suggests they all dine on bread and fish. He provides. The meal Jesus offers and eats is a characteristically simple meal in two ways. First, the food itself is simple. This healthy supper of bread and fish is probably the most common menu for Jesus and his disciples and for the families gathered to hear him that day. A second aspect of simplicity is that Jesus, in preparing the meal, uses what is available. While the disciples assume that having enough requires extravagant expenditure, Jesus knows that what is already available is adequate.

This meal of fish and bread feeds five thousand men and all the women and children accompanying them. Not only does everyone eat until full; the disciples collect twelve baskets of leftovers. On another occasion, Jesus similarly provides a meal of bread and fish to a slightly smaller crowd—four thousand men and their families (Matthew 15:32-39). This time Jesus has seven loaves and a few fish as he begins to provide the meal. Although he starts with more food and feeds a smaller crowd, only seven baskets of leftovers are collected. This smaller crowd, however, has been in the desert listening to Jesus for three days!

In another example—this one from a postresurrection story—Jesus and some of his disciples are once again dining on bread and fish (John 21:4-14). Surely this was a typical meal for them. In this story, Jesus again provides. After helping the disciples with some fishing advice, Jesus becomes the chef at an early morning fish fry. He grills the bread and fish over a charcoal fire and then serves the meal.

We can conclude that Jesus and his disciples most often ate simple, healthy meals such as bread and fish. Tending the body with food, however, is about more than what you eat. Even choosing healthy food is not sufficient. *How* you eat is also important. Eating your meal in the car while driving to work, at the desk in the office, or in front of the television late at night may not contribute to a healthy body. Return to Luke's account of this huge picnic. Look more carefully at how Jesus organizes the event.

Jesus tells the disciples to "make them sit down in groups of about fifty each" (Luke 9:14). We read that the disciples do just that, making everyone sit down in a group. Now think for a moment about how *we* might stage this large meal for thousands of people. What would be the most efficient strategy? We could set up five stations with two disciples at each station—one with bread, one with fish. Tell everyone to get in a line. Our two "extra" disciples can help direct traffic to even out the lines. Folks wait in line to pick up their food. Some will quickly get back in a different line to get second helpings. Some will eat before leaving. Others may pack the food to eat as they begin their journey home. Since no evening session is planned, the entire crowd will soon begin to disperse. But that is not the scene here. Jesus tells the people to get in groups and sit down. They gather, sitting with family, friends, and neighbors who have been standing nearby throughout the day. They have a time of fellowship. No doubt they have a lot to talk about, having spent the day with Jesus.

Perhaps this story provides instruction for us beyond the example of eating healthy food. Jesus says to get in a group and sit down. So, gather for a meal with family, friends, and guests. Sit around a table or on the floor or in the grass. Sit close enough to look in the faces of the others. Talk and listen; ask questions and give responses. Relax your body; engage your mind; open your heart and soul to know the others sharing the meal and to be known yourself. The fellowship around the table may be as important as the food itself. Pause to give thanks for the food and for one another. Jesus broke and shared bread and fish. But, perhaps cutting a cheese pizza—a common food on many of our tables—putting a hot slice on a plate, and passing it provides a similar experience of sharing a common, simple food.

Jesus probably joined all the others that day by sitting down and eating bread and fish. He tended his body in what he ate. He tended his body—and his heart, mind, and soul, as well—in the *way* he ate his food. By following the example of the meal for five thousand, we may discover that ordinary bread—whether a crusty loaf of sourdough, a slice of sandwich bread, a pita, or pizza crust—becomes the bread of life that nurtures our whole being. May we gather, sit down, bless, break, and share. In the desert that day, the thousands of people "all ate and were filled" (Luke 9:17). Perhaps if we are attentive to how we eat as well as to what we eat, more than our stomachs may be filled and satisfied.

Exercise

How did Jesus tend his body? Jesus walked. Did he walk because his doctor had advised him that walking was the best exercise to care for his heart? Did Jesus need to walk every day to get in the required steps or recommended mileage? Of course not! Unlike today when people set aside special time to exercise as an end in itself, Jesus walked out of necessity to accomplish his mission. Reading the Gospels, one quickly gets a sense of the constant movement of Jesus from place to place. Not only did he walk mile after mile; Jesus frequently climbed mountains as well. What a challenge this must have been for many of his disciples! The fishermen among them were, no doubt, strong from the rigors of their work, but even they may not have been prepared for the long walks day after day. For others—the tax collector Matthew, for example—the task of following may have presented an immediate physical challenge. Whether intentional or not, a result of Jesus' exercise, and that of his disciples, was vigor and endurance. Jesus tended his physical health with considerable exercise. Following his example, at whatever level we are capable of doing, is certainly wise for us, as well.

To do what he needed to do, Jesus had to be physically fit. To get where he needed to go, Jesus chose the mode of travel most readily available to him: walking. Is this, however, the whole truth? Did Jesus have other choices? Did Jesus need to take the journeys he took—and take them in the way that he did? Crowds heard Jesus and then told others about him. Crowds followed him, even when he tried to escape from them. Jesus did not need to travel from place to place to find people to heal and people to listen to his teaching. He could have set up headquarters in a synagogue in one of the major cities and done all his preaching and teaching from there, expecting people to come to him. On the other hand, perhaps a wealthy patron could have given Jesus a horse to ride. He did have some followers with resources to provide for his needs. Jesus could have saved so much time traveling from place to place if he had acquired an animal to ride. He also could have escaped the crowds so much more easily if only he could have moved faster than the people. Didn't Jesus think of these advantages? Why did Jesus walk when he could have stayed put or moved faster? Jesus' own thoughts and his conversations with his disciples about such practical matters are generally not recorded in the Gospels. We can, however, speculate on why he did what he did.

Perhaps Jesus was tending more than his body. Walking not only directly strengthens the heart muscles and other parts of the body, but it also aids the body by relieving stress and tension. Did Jesus experience stress? Look at how often Jesus debated the Pharisees, enduring their attacks and their constant plots to trap him. Consider the times when Jesus taught and healed and preached for hours, even days. When he needed to get away from the crowd, often he escaped only to be found by them again. Perhaps the walking helped Jesus cope with all he faced. As he walked, he could talk about the day with his disciples. Sometimes Jesus walked ahead of the others, giving him time to think through events of the day on his own. Walking helped Jesus tend his body. It may have helped him tend his heart, mind, and soul as well.

Another benefit of walking is a direct result of the slower pace: it allows one to notice and to be available to other persons along the way. Compare walking to a neighborhood school to accompany your child home at the end of the school day, to driving there in your car. Yes, the trip will take much longer on foot, but how many more persons might you have the opportunity to see and talk to—persons you would miss if you were traveling much faster in the car? What conversation might you have with your child given the leisurely pace of a walk that you would miss in the brief car ride?

Walking along the road made Jesus available to people who needed him. In John 9:1 we read, "As he walked along, he saw a man blind from birth." Jesus healed this man of his blindness. On another occasion, "As Jesus was walking along, he saw a man called Matthew sitting at the tax booth" (Matthew 9:9). Here Jesus met a man who needed a new calling and a new life. In this same man, Jesus found someone to help him in his ministry. Again, walking provided opportunities beyond its health benefits.

Although Jesus could have established his ministry in one location, his choice to travel throughout the region was intentional. Jesus' message was not only for those who could come to him. He wanted to reach out to all people, including the helpless, the excluded, and the despised. At times, the mere act of walking into a region, as when Jesus went to Gadara (Matthew 8:28) or through Samaria (John 4:4-5), made a statement of inclusion. Some people would not have known they were invited to the kingdom Jesus was proclaiming had he not taken the invitation directly to them.

Even so, walking was a slow mode of travel and an inefficient way for Jesus to spread his message. Perhaps, however, walking was part of the message. Jesus' decision to walk everywhere was consistent with his simple lifestyle. "Foxes have holes, and birds of the air have nests; but the Son of Man has nowhere to lay his head" (Luke 9:58). Jesus could not be burdened with feeding and sheltering horses. He modeled what he instructed his disciples to do when he sent them out as missionaries: "Take nothing for your journey" (Luke 9:3). Jesus' decision to walk from place to place also was consistent with his humility. Jesus walked to the people as a servant coming to serve. He did not ride in, impressing the poor and lowly with horses or camels. How he came said something about who he was.

Hour after hour, mile after mile, Jesus walked. He tended his body with healthy exercise. The walking helped tend his mind, heart, and soul as well. The walking revealed a lifestyle and humility uncharacteristic of many of the religious teachers and leaders of his day.

If we are to follow Jesus, we must be strong and fit enough to do all God is calling us to do. If we are to follow Jesus, we must go where the excluded ones live in our society. We must go simply and humbly as those coming to walk along beside our sisters and brothers. "As Jesus was walking along . . . he said . . . 'Follow me'" (Matthew 9:9). So also he walks along and says to us, "Follow me."

"As He Rode Along"

When he had come near Bethphage and Bethany, at the place called the Mount of Olives, he sent two of the disciples, saying, "Go into the village ahead of you, and as you enter it you will find tied there a colt that has never been ridden. Untie it and bring it here. If anyone asks you, 'Why are you untying it?' just say this, 'The Lord needs it.'" So those who were sent departed and found it as he had told them. As they were untying the colt, its owners asked them, "Why are you untying the colt?" They said, "The Lord needs it." Then they brought it to Jesus; and after throwing their cloaks on the colt, they set Jesus on it. As he rode along, people kept spreading their cloaks on the road. As he was now approaching the path down from the Mount of Olives, the whole multitude of the disciples began to praise God joyfully with a loud voice for all the deeds of power that they had seen, saying,

> *"Blessed is the king*
> *who comes in the name of the Lord!*
> *Peace in heaven,*
> *and glory in the highest heaven!" (Luke 19:29-38)*

Throughout his ministry, Jesus walked. Day after day, mile after mile, Jesus and his followers walked from village to village, preaching, teaching, and healing. Occasionally, Jesus and his disciples took a boat across the Sea of Galilee. Otherwise, the gospel accounts say that always they walked—except for this one time. When he entered Jerusalem on this occasion, Jesus rode a donkey.

All four gospel writers recorded this event. It was a scene unlike any other in Jesus' ministry. Often he drew a crowd and attracted considerable attention. On several occasions, Jesus was honored with banquets and feasts. Only this time, however, was such adulation directed at Jesus. Cloaks were thrown across the donkey and spread in the street ahead. According to the writer of the Gospel of John, the people carried palm branches—presumably to spread on the ground or wave in honor of Jesus—and shouted "Hosanna!" (12:13). This was indeed a grand entrance into Jerusalem. This one time, Jesus did not walk. Although he chose to ride a donkey, a humble animal, rather than a fine horse, it was a big celebration of and for Jesus. This entrance was not as simple and did not appear as humble as Jesus' entrances into all the other towns over the past three years. Why did Jesus ride the donkey?

Although neither Mark nor Luke makes specific reference to prophecy, both Matthew (21:5) and John (12:15) refer to words from the prophet Zechariah: "Lo, your king comes to you; triumphant and victorious is he, / humble and riding on a donkey, / on a colt, the foal of a donkey" (9:9b). The details of the entrance into Jerusalem suggest the fulfillment of this prophecy. The people in Jerusalem were indeed shouting. Jesus was in fact riding a young donkey. Nevertheless, the event is worthy of our reflection apart from prophecy. In the context of Jesus' entire ministry, this event is exceptional. The people were shouting praises for Jesus, celebrating him as king in the tradition of David. Jesus did not attempt to correct them or to clarify his mission. He did not refuse the cloaks and branches spread before him. He did not walk into Jerusalem. He rode.

Indeed, this was a special day. The crowd gathered to praise and to welcome him; the disciples arriving with him may have thought this day was the beginning of a new day, a new kingdom. Jesus would be king. Some Jews that day may have hoped for a political king like David, a king who would overthrow the oppressive Roman rule. Others may have thought Jesus would overthrow the oppression of the Pharisees and other religious leaders. Whatever the beliefs of all gathered there, they shared a moment of expectation. Perhaps Jesus, too, was sharing in this celebration, not expecting to triumph as king but celebrating the hope of the triumph of the kingdom of God he had preached.

Consider for a moment another special day of hope: a wedding day. A young bride and groom are being married, a couple with simple tastes from families with simple means. They are far more concerned with what is said and what is pledged than with decorations and attire. Yet, when the newlyweds emerge from the church to go to the reception, a limousine is waiting. Later, they will leave for their honeymoon in the groom's seven-year-old car. But, for this special first ride as husband and wife, the short trip will be unique and memorable. The families and friends gathered celebrate the moment that is made even more special because of what is, for them, extravagant and extraordinary. The limosine is part of the celebration of hope that all the joy and love expressed that day will be fulfilled in the days and years to come. The bride and groom have never ridden in a limousine. They may never do so again. But for this one trip on this one special day, riding in that car is the right thing to do. Riding in it is what those who love them want them to do. The newlyweds feel honored and loved as they ride in it.

Perhaps for the shouting crowd in Jerusalem, for the twelve disciples, and even for Jesus himself, riding that donkey was the right thing for Jesus to do.

Jesus did not live his life following a rule book. He tended his body with healthy eating and exercise. He dined simply on bread and fish, occasionally accepting invitations to banquets. He walked everywhere, all the time, except just once when he rode a donkey. Jesus recognized that celebrations, even extravagant celebrations, were sometimes the right thing to do. Jesus tended his heart, mind, and soul by riding that donkey into Jerusalem that day. Moments later, he would cry over Jerusalem. He would enter the temple and drive out money changers. There he also would find sick and blind persons still waiting to be healed. Before all this, as he rode along, he was filled with hope.

Jesus led a simple lifestyle, yet he joined in celebrations—even extravagant ones. His example is an invitation to us to celebrate special occasions of hope—weddings, graduations, anniversaries, new job or retirement parties, and other celebrations. May the "ride instead of walk" image help us choose memorable celebrations that will help tend body, heart, mind, and soul.

Rest

Jesus tended his body by resting when he needed to rest and by sleeping when he needed to sleep. When we focus only on Jesus' teaching, preaching, and healing, we may overlook this fact. Consider, for example, the events described in Matthew 8. A crowd had been following Jesus. He had healed three people: a leper, the servant of a centurion, and Peter's mother-in-law. Then we read: "Now when Jesus saw great crowds around him, he gave orders to go over to the other side. . . . And when he got into the boat, his disciples followed him. A windstorm arose on the sea, so great that the boat was being swamped by the waves; but he was asleep" (Matthew 8:18, 23-24). The terrified disciples woke Jesus. We pay attention to the frightened disciples and to Jesus as he calmed the wind and the sea. We consider this powerful act, described as a miracle, and answer for ourselves the question asked by the disciples about the identity of this man. Look, however, at his humanity. Jesus needed to renew his strength. So, even though the crowd was still gathered around to hear his preaching and to witness his healing, Jesus left them. He escaped to the boat. He went to sleep, even as the storm raged.

Jesus did get tired. He did not ignore the need for rest. He did not try to keep on until he had nothing more to give. Several times in the Gospels we read that Jesus left the crowd before they were ready for him to leave (e.g., Matthew 14:22; 15:39). He withdrew to a boat, to a mountain, or to some other deserted place. Toward the end of his ministry, after arriving in Jerusalem, Jesus escaped the city in the evening, withdrawing, we may assume, to reflect, rest, and sleep. In his record of the week in Jerusalem, Matthew writes of Jesus being in the temple driving out the money changers, healing the sick, and responding to the criticism of the chief priests and the scribes. Then, "He left them, went out of the city to Bethany, and spent the night there" (Matthew 21:17). Jesus always prepared himself for whatever he faced. This time, rest was part of the necessary preparation for the events of the coming days in Jerusalem.

Jesus knew his followers needed to rest, too. An example is recorded in the Gospel of Mark. Jesus sent his disciples out as missionaries. We read, "So they went out and proclaimed that all should repent. They cast out many demons, and anointed with oil many who were sick and cured them" (Mark 6:12-13). When the disciples returned, they went to Jesus and gave him a report on all they had done. What happened next should not be overlooked. "[Jesus] said to them, 'Come away to a deserted place all by yourselves and rest a while.' For many were coming and going, and they had no leisure even to eat. And they went away in the boat to a deserted place by themselves" (Mark 6:31-32).

Here Jesus recognized the need for rest, not only for the body, but also for the heart, mind, and soul. He sent his disciples on retreat to rest and reflect on where they had been and what they had done. The much needed retreat was delayed, however. The writer of Mark recorded that the crowd saw that Jesus and the disciples had left on the boat. So the crowd ran around the lake on land to get there ahead of them. Jesus had compassion on the crowd and took time to teach and feed them. But, after that, once again Jesus sent his disciples off to rest. Instead of the gentle invitation to rest given earlier, this time we read that Jesus *made* them get on the boat and go (Mark 6:45).

Twice that we know of, at least three of the disciples—Peter, James, and John—were heavy with sleep. The first time, Jesus had taken these three up a mountain with him to pray. Jesus' face and his clothes were glowing white; he was talking with Moses and Elijah. The writer of Luke records that Peter, James, and John "were weighed down with sleep," but that "they had stayed awake" (Luke 9:32). Why were these three men so sleepy? Look at what they almost missed because of their fatigue!

The second time that we know Peter, James, and John were sleepy, they missed one of the most intimate and passionate moments in Jesus' ministry. This time, in Gethsemane before his betrayal, Jesus rebuked these disciples three times for falling asleep after he had asked them to pray with him. Jesus had tended his body in preparation for what he was facing. He needed to be alert to pray so that he could prepare his heart, mind, and soul, as well. The disciples, however, were not adequately prepared for this night. Yes, their day had been long and filled with heavy emotion. They had just finished the Passover meal, and the weight of the emotion and the food and wine could have made their eyes heavy. Whatever their reasons, they were sleeping when they needed to be awake, perhaps because they had been awake when they needed to sleep.

In much of our society, rest and sleep are not highly valued. Most job descriptions call for forty hours of work a week; however, many bosses expect fifty hours while others in the office are working sixty. How can we rest when facing such expectations and job competition? When parents work full time and their children have numerous after-school activities to attend and all the household chores need to be done, who can hope to get eight or seven or even six hours of sleep every night? Students need to study. Caregivers are needed twenty-four hours a day. How can we rest when others might think we are just plain lazy or weak or unwilling to do our share of the work?

Look at Jesus; consider his work. Jesus had important things to do, too. Surely that is an understatement! Yet, Jesus knew that physical strength was required to do what he was called to do. So, when he was tired, he rested.

Jesus frequently stopped his work so that he could rest. He knew that rest is not for the body alone. Tending heart, mind, and soul is made more difficult if the body is tired. Jesus needed rest to have the strength for the discipline of prayer. He needed to pray to renew heart, mind, and soul so that he might be what God called him to be and do what God called him to do. Jesus told his followers to rest as well.

Think about what we may miss if we are too tired to hear the voice of God. Jesus' words are to all of us: "Come away . . . and rest a while" (Mark 6:31).

"Tired Out by His Journey"

Now when Jesus learned that the Pharisees had heard, "Jesus is making and baptizing more disciples than John"—although it was not Jesus himself but his disciples who baptized—he left Judea and started back to Galilee. But he had to go through Samaria. So he came to a Samaritan city called Sychar, near the plot of ground that Jacob had given to his son Joseph. Jacob's well was there, and Jesus, tired out by his journey, was sitting by the well. It was about noon. (John 4:1-6)

Jesus was "tired out." The story about Jesus' encounter with the Samaritan woman follows this text. While that story is very familiar, this phrase is not among those memorized by children in Sunday school. We may gloss over such descriptions, sometimes spiritualizing them to make Jesus seem less human and more divine. The text does not suggest that Jesus went through Samaria and to the well just to encounter that woman. Jesus went through Samaria because "he had to" (v. 4). He was not faking fatigue, nor was he staging the meeting with the woman. Jesus was exhausted. He needed to sit down and rest. He was thirsty, too. Jesus asked the woman for a drink of water (v. 7). Yes, this need for rest and water presented an opportunity to meet the Samaritan woman and talk about living water, but it is important to note that the whole episode began with Jesus' physical need for rest.

"It was about noon" when Jesus sat down to rest (v. 6). The gospel writer reports that "his disciples had gone to the city to buy food" (v. 8). The disciples, possibly complaining that they were hungry, most likely wanted Jesus to go with them to the city; but they went on without him. When they returned with lunch, the disciples urged Jesus, saying, "Rabbi, eat something" (v. 31b). Just about noon was the time to eat lunch. The time to rest was following that meal during the mid-afternoon heat of the day. Perhaps the disciples fussed at Jesus for stopping to rest in Samaria. After all, the people there were considered "unclean" by Jewish religious leaders. We may speculate that the disciples considered this to be the wrong place and the wrong time to rest. Jesus, however, listened to his body. He was tired out. He rested.

Jesus' lifestyle reveals a seemingly simple pattern—rest when you are tired; eat when you are hungry. How much of our own physical distress is caused by not resting when we are exhausted or not eating when we are hungry—or eating when we are *not* hungry?

Look more closely at Jesus' tending of his own needs. Perhaps in resting by the well while the disciples went to town, he was listening not only to his body but also to his heart and soul. Again we read that Jesus was "tired out by his journey" (v. 6). Had the walking from Judea been more exhausting for him than for his companions? Perhaps, but consider also the reason for the trip. Apparently, some controversy had been aroused with the Pharisees because of the number of people being baptized to be followers of Jesus. Being at the center of hostility can be as exhausting as physical exercise—sometimes more so. Jesus' "journey" could refer not only to the miles he had walked but also to the path he had followed in pursuing his calling. Perhaps opposition from the Pharisees had worn him out. Jesus' fatigue might have been as much from emotional stress as from all that walking. In any case, Jesus needed rest—the rest of sitting down by the well and being quiet.

While Jesus was resting, the Samaritan woman came to the well to draw water. The opportunity to ask for a drink of water became an opportunity to talk about God. Rather than deplete his spirit, the conversation more likely was refreshing. Unlike the draining controversy that he had faced with the Pharisees, this exchange appears to have been encouraging. The woman was open to listening to Jesus and to receiving his message about God. In fact, she became an instant missionary, going to tell family and friends about Jesus.

The idea that the encounter with the woman filled and refreshed Jesus is suggested by his conversation with his disciples when they returned with lunch. When Jesus refused the food they urged him to eat, the disciples speculated that someone else had already given him food. Jesus corrected them, saying, "My food is to do the will of him who sent me and to complete his work" (John 4:34). When Jesus was hungry for food, he would eat. For now, a deeper hunger had been satisfied. If knowledge of the rising opposition among the Pharisees had emptied him, then perhaps inviting and receiving this woman as a follower had filled him.

Jesus said, "Come to me, all you that are weary and are carrying heavy burdens, and I will give you rest" (Matthew 11:28). The woman had the heavy burden of her water jar and the heavier burden of a heart and soul weighted down by her life experiences. She found deep rest in being with and knowing Jesus. She would not have received that gift, however, had Jesus not practiced what he preached. Because Jesus stopped to rest when he was tired and because he engaged this woman at the well, not only the woman but also "many Samaritans from that city believed in him" (John 4:39). Jesus and his disciples stayed a few days in Samaria before continuing to Galilee. No doubt he left there renewed in body and spirit because he knew he needed to rest when he was all "tired out."

Touch

Jesus recognized the importance of touch in tending the body. Most evident throughout his ministry was the significance of touch in healing.

For example, in Matthew 8 and 9, Jesus touched several people: the leper who was made clean, Peter's mother-in-law who was made well, the girl who was brought back to life, and the blind men who were made to see. The healing touch of Jesus was not some required ritual, not some gesture of a magic act. Rather, through the physical connection of touch, power went out of Jesus into the one needing healing. Often Jesus extended his hand to make that connection. At other times, persons who needed healing reached out to touch Jesus. In Mark 5:25-34, we read of the woman with hemorrhages touching only the cloak Jesus wore. Yet, Jesus felt the power leave him. In Luke 6:19 we read, "And all in the crowd were trying to touch him, for power came out from him and healed all of them."

No one can explain fully, and certainly no one can match, the healing power attributed to Jesus. Even so, clinical research has proved the therapeutic value of human touch. For example, holding and stroking premature infants is now practiced in hospitals because of the benefits of human touch for these babies. Also, many practices in nontraditional medicine use touch to treat pain and other problems.

The healing offered by Jesus when he touched someone usually went deeper than the physical ailment. Jesus' touch communicated acceptance, establishing a physical connection with healing potential beyond the curing of disease. When he touched the leper, going against religious laws about what was clean or unclean, Jesus broke social and religious barriers to say without words that the person was accepted and included in God's family.

The touch of Jesus was not only a conduit of healing power and acceptance but also of blessings. In the Gospel of Mark we read of women bringing their children to Jesus so that he might touch them and bless them. After rebuking the disciples for trying to keep the children away, Jesus "took them up in his arms, laid his hands on them, and blessed them" (Mark 10:16). What a gentle yet powerful scene. Jesus used touch to bless and to affirm the value of the least of these, including children and others who had no status in that society.

Jesus' touch also soothed, calmed, and comforted the body—and perhaps the heart, as well. At the transfiguration, Peter, James, and John heard the voice from a cloud naming Jesus as Son. They were terrified and fell down on the ground. In Matthew we read one account of what happened next: "Jesus came and touched them, saying 'Get up and do not be afraid' " (17:7).

Thus, Jesus' touch offered to others many different gifts. Healing power flowed through his touch—hand to hand, hand to eyes, hand to garment. He offered blessing through his touch. His touch symbolized acceptance, the breaking down of religious and cultural barriers. The comfort provided through his touch could calm the storm within any person. If we assume, however, that Jesus only gave the gift of touch, that he had no need to receive any of what he offered others, then we are mistaken.

Jesus was touched by others, allowing them to tend him. One of the most passionate accounts of Jesus being tended by another person took place in the home of Simon, a Pharisee. Jesus had been invited there to share a meal. The significant event of that evening is vividly described in the Gospel of Luke: "And a woman in the city, who was a sinner, having learned that he was eating in the Pharisee's house, brought an alabaster jar of ointment. She stood behind him at his feet, weeping, and began to bathe his feet with her tears and to dry them with her hair. Then she continued kissing his feet and anointing them with the ointment" (7:37-38). Simon criticized Jesus for allowing this act from this woman whom the Pharisee called "a sinner." In turn, Jesus criticized his host for not showing hospitality. The woman not only washed Jesus' feet but also kissed and anointed them with oil. Simon had neglected washing, kissing, and anointing. The woman's touch comforted and soothed Jesus' body. Perhaps her anointing with oil was a form of blessing to him, and her tears and touch a source of healing to his bruised spirit.

Jesus valued the healing power of touch. His actions revealed this over and over again. The scene at Simon's house shows us that Jesus valued touch not only for others but for himself, as well. After defending to his critical host the actions of the woman with the alabaster jar, Jesus said, "She has shown great love" (Luke 7:47). That is what a touch can be: a touch of love. We see this woman tending Jesus' body, yet these words of Jesus tell us that she touched his heart as well. Jesus' call to us is this: Go and share the healing power of the touch of love.

"Reclining Next to Him"

Jesus was troubled in spirit, and declared, "Very truly, I tell you, one of you will betray me." The disciples looked at one another, uncertain of whom he was speaking. One of his disciples—the one whom Jesus loved—was reclining next to him; Simon Peter therefore motioned to him to ask Jesus of whom he was speaking. So while reclining next to Jesus, he asked him, "Lord, who is it?" (John 13:21-25)

In the Gospel of John, the Passover meal is described differently from the accounts in the Synoptic Gospels. Instead of telling us that Jesus and his disciples shared the bread and the cup, the writer of John tells us that Jesus washed the feet of his disciples and talked about being a servant to others (13:1-20). Then Jesus made a clear statement that one of the disciples gathered with him would betray him (v. 21). One disciple, identified first here and again at the cross and in post-resurrection events, is not mentioned by his proper name but is named in a very special way as "the one whom Jesus loved" (v. 23). The text tells us that he was reclining next to Jesus. Peter would later refer to this exact moment while talking with the postresurrection Jesus. We read, "Peter turned and saw the disciple whom Jesus loved following them; he was the one who had reclined next to Jesus at the supper and had said, 'Lord, who is it that is going to betray you?'" (21:20).

Let us look at this disciple who was reclining next to Jesus. First, we may recall that reclining on the floor, perhaps on cushions, was a common practice. We have seen pictures of Greeks and Romans of that era doing so. This one disciple, however, had a special place and relationship with Jesus. In the King James Version, the disciple is described as "leaning on Jesus' bosom" (13:23) and as "lying on Jesus' breast" (13:25). The picture and feel is one of relaxed intimacy between this disciple and Jesus.

Have you ever reclined next to someone—spouse, parent, child, close friend? Probably the relationship with the other person was such that you were at ease, comfortable hanging out together. Maybe the two of you were watching television, talking, reading books, or dozing. Leaning on someone does tend the body. The experience can be relaxing, calming, and comforting. Reclining next to another can feel safe, warm, and affirming.

That a disciple was reclining next to Jesus is not remarkable. However, this particular disciple, called "the one whom Jesus loved," was singled out as having a special relationship with Jesus. Of course, Jesus loved all of his disciples, but something about the relationship with this one was different.

Many times in the gospel stories we read of three disciples accompanying Jesus for extraordinary experiences. Peter, James, and John were with Jesus when he was transfigured. Those three were also with Jesus in the garden of Gethsemane, praying just before Jesus' arrest. Other gospel accounts seem to indicate that Peter had a closer relationship with Jesus than some of the disciples. Peter was the one who walked on the water—or tried to—to meet Jesus. Peter was the one Jesus named as the foundation for his church. But at the Passover meal, Peter did not ask Jesus the hard question. Peter motioned to this other disciple to ask Jesus who would betray him. Perhaps Peter did not want to ask from his position farther away from Jesus, not wanting the other disciples to hear. Or perhaps Peter was not quite confident enough or comfortable enough to ask Jesus such a dark and difficult question. He would let the one whom Jesus loved, the one reclining next to him, ask the question. This other man did not hesitate to ask.

What we may learn about tending from this passage goes beyond, or beneath, the mere physical aspect of tending the body with touch. In order for touch to tend, certain characteristics must exist in the relationship. Honesty, trust, and respect—each for the other—are required. A caring and loving spirit is also needed. In this case, Jesus knew and loved the disciple next to him, just as the disciple knew and loved Jesus in return.

Such deep love is not always necessary, however, for touch to be effective. A physician can sit with and hold the hand of a hurting and frightened patient and, by doing so, tend the body. A pastor can tend a grieving parishioner with a compassionate embrace. A teacher can tend the body of a crying child by carefully cleaning and bandaging a cut. In each of these cases, as in the case of Jesus and his beloved disciple leaning against him, more than the body may be tended. A tending touch may comfort not only the physical, beating heart but also the emotional heart.

Perhaps as Jesus despaired that one would betray him, he was comforted by the hope that this one against his breast would stay with him.

While in the Synoptic Gospels the disciples all fled and were absent from the crucifixion, in John's Gospel this disciple whom Jesus loved was present at the cross. Jesus even entrusted the care of his mother to this disciple.

After the Passover meal, later in the evening, Jesus would receive touches that would not tend his body. Judas would kiss him in an act of betrayal. Representatives from the chief priests would lay hands on him and arrest him. Later still, Jesus would be slapped and beaten. But for this brief time, Jesus' body was lovingly tended by the one reclining next to him whom he loved.

Questions for Reflection and Discussion

1. How does the way we see and treat our bodies affect our relationship with God? with others?
2. Make a list of things that tend and nurture the body. Which of these do you regularly practice? How might you better tend your own body?
3. What foods do you eat at a typical meal? Evaluate how healthy this meal is for your body. Then evaluate how this meal affects your life in other ways—emotions, stress, comfort, expense. What one change in your eating habits might you make to better tend your body?
4. During a typical week, how many meals do you eat sitting around a table with family and friends? Where else and how else do you eat other meals? Compare how you feel after a meal of the first type versus the second type. How do your mealtime habits—time of day, length of time spent at the meal, atmosphere or setting—affect the health of your body? Of your whole self?
5. We need to be the healthiest we can be to do what we are called to do. What does Jesus' example tell us about the need for exercise? Why do you think this is an area where so many people struggle? What adjustments might you need to make in order to be the healthiest you can be in this area of your life?
6. How many hours of sleep do you get each night? How many hours do you think you need? What are some of the effects of

fatigue on your work and your relationships? How is the balance among rest, work, play, and exercise in your life right now? What changes might you need to make in order to tend your body in healthier ways?

7. Cultural influences may affect how we tend our bodies with food, exercise, rest, and touch. Identify several of these cultural influences, and consider whether each is healthy or unhealthy. If unhealthy, what action can be taken to counteract this influence?

8. Reflect on an experience of healing, comforting touch. What made that experience healing and comforting for you? Too often we read and hear stories about the abuse of touch in our society. What are some ways we can ensure or reclaim safe, healing touch for ourselves or for others?

2. Tending the Heart

H OW DID JESUS TEND HIS HEART? BEFORE WE CAN ANSWER THAT QUES-
tion, we must reflect on what we mean by *heart*. If we take that word
literally, we may once again think about diet, exercise, cholesterol, and
stress tests. Our understanding of the heart, however, encompasses
more than a vital organ of the body. Jesus speaks about at least three
aspects of the heart: condition, function or activity, and location.
Perhaps by considering Jesus' words about each of these aspects we
can better understand the meaning of *heart* in the Gospels.

Describing a possible condition of the heart, Jesus says that the "pure
in heart" will see God (Matthew 5:8). In the parable of the Sower, he
teaches that those who are like the good soil will hear the word and
hold it "in an honest and good heart" (Luke 8:15). In contrast, those
whose hearts are hardened—including the Pharisees (Mark 3:5) and, at
times, the disciples (Mark 6:52)—do not understand or do not accept
Jesus and his teaching. In other examples, Jesus talks about the heart
being troubled (John 14:1) or afraid (Mark 6:50b). Another description
of the condition of the heart comes from the men on the road to
Emmaus, who, when they recognize that they had been with Jesus, say
that their hearts were burning within them (Luke 24:32). Thus, the
condition of our hearts affects what we hear, or, at least, how we hear
and what we understand.

The men going to Emmaus not only describe a condition of the
heart, but they also suggest one function or role of the heart: percep-
tion or intuition. We will see later the vital role of the mind in our
thinking and deciding, but we read in the Gospels that the heart also
has a role in these activities. For example, in parallel texts about Jesus
forgiving the sins of the paralyzed man before healing him, Jesus
asks the scribes why they "think evil" (Matthew 9:4) or "raise such

questions" (Mark 2:8) in their hearts. Another function of the heart is to hold and to express our emotions. If we are fearful, for example, we experience that in our heart. Similarly, an important activity of the heart, yet not the heart alone, is loving. The "greatest commandment" begins with "You shall love the Lord your God with all your heart" (Luke 10:27).

A third aspect of the heart, its location, is also important for our understanding of the Gospels' view of *heart*. In Matthew 6:21, Jesus makes this simple statement: "For where your treasure is, there your heart will be also." Often in his teaching and storytelling, as well as in his encounters with others, Jesus comments on the effects of being attached to things other than God. He warns, for example, of having a primary attachment to wealth. Jesus suggests such attachments reflect where we have put our heart.

What, then, can we conclude about the meaning of heart? The heart is one key to our understanding of what we hear, of what we see, and of the people and situations we encounter. It holds and expresses our emotions. It contributes an emotional dimension to our decisions. The heart follows what we value and binds us to that treasure. Given this, how might we tend our hearts? We can take care how we deal with and express our emotions. We can admit what we treasure and assess the consequences of those choices. And we can nurture healthy, close relationships with others. The reflections that follow offer insights and examples regarding how Jesus tended his heart in each of these ways.

Anger

One of the emotions most destructive to the heart—both the physical and emotional heart—is anger. How did Jesus tend his anger? Perhaps we believe that he did not get angry. We may think anger is too negative an emotion for Jesus—or perhaps even a sin. Actually, feeling anger and even expressing anger need not be equated with sinful acts. Anger may be sinful when it is held in such a way that it is self-destructive or is unleashed in a way that is destructive of someone else. Nevertheless, most of us are far more comfortable labeling as "righteous indignation" anything Jesus said or did that seems to approach anger. Before we add, "Do not be angry" to our list of commandments, we need to look again at Jesus and listen to his words.

The most dramatic example of an outburst from Jesus is a familiar story. The event is recorded in all four gospels:

> The Passover of the Jews was near, and Jesus went up to Jerusalem. In the temple he found people selling cattle, sheep, and doves, and the money changers seated at their tables. Making a whip of cords, he drove all of them out of the temple, both the sheep and the cattle. He also poured out the coins of the money changers and overturned their tables. He told those who were selling the doves, "Take these things out of here! Stop making my Father's house a marketplace!" (John 2:13-16)

Jesus did get angry. Here he expressed his anger immediately and directly, and his response was appropriate to the situation. He confronted the "cattle auction" in the temple and took the action he thought necessary, even if it risked his personal safety. He drove money changers and sellers of animals out of the temple and, according to Matthew's account, he then turned his attention to healing those who sought him in the temple (21:14).

Jesus often expressed his anger toward the religious leaders—scribes, Pharisees, and others. When challenged about plucking grain to eat on the Sabbath, Jesus asked the Pharisees, "Have you not read what David did?" (Matthew 12:3). Surely this offended the religious leaders. Can you imagine asking your own pastor after the Sunday morning sermon if he or she had read the scripture text? Jesus was angry and, no doubt, made the religious leaders angry, too. Yet he was appropriate and clear, and he had a constructive purpose. Jesus tried to get the Pharisees to read beyond the letter of the law so that they might understand more clearly who God is and the kind of relationship God desires.

In the Gospel of Mark, we read that on the same Sabbath, Jesus entered the synagogue where he saw a man with a withered hand. Again the Pharisees were there, waiting to see if Jesus would break Sabbath laws. We know Jesus' mood this time. The author writes that Jesus "looked around at them with anger" (Mark 3:5). Jesus defied them and healed the man.

On several occasions Jesus returned the challenge and argued with the Pharisees, such as when he was accused of healing "by Beelzebul" (Matthew 12:22-28). Even more sharply, Jesus challenged the Pharisees when they questioned the washing practices of his disciples, firing back critically, "Why do you break the commandment of God for the sake of your tradition?" (Matthew 15:1-3). At times Jesus' anger could be heard in his name-calling—accurate and appropriate, though name-calling nonetheless. For example, he called the Pharisees and other religious leaders "hypocrites" (Mark 7:6), "blind guides" (Matthew 23:16), and "fools" (Luke 11:40).

Of course, Jesus did not always respond in anger when provoked. When Jesus was frustrated by the unbelief of those who heard him, for example, he often responded without angry words. Rather than allowing frustration to turn into unproductive anger, Jesus simply walked away. For example, when rejected by his hometown, he left and "went on his way" (Luke 4:16-30). The gospel writer's words suggest that Jesus immediately, calmly, and without anger moved on to do the work he needed to do. Likewise, when the Pharisees asked for a sign after signs had been given, Jesus "sighed deeply. . . . And he left them" (Mark 8:11, 13). Jesus may have perceived that the hometown folks who knew him and the Pharisees who had already seen signs were determined not to be persuaded by or satisfied with anything he could say or do. Perhaps he knew that his anger would be futile and might cause his opponents to dig in their heels even more deeply against him. In any case, he simply moved on.

Jesus' anger was directed not only at those labeled his enemies, but also at his disciples. Sometimes Jesus' words to his disciples sounded very impatient, perhaps deeply disappointed as well, and possibly even angry. For example, when the disciples failed to understand Jesus' parables and teachings (Mark 4:13; 7:18), or when they seemed to lack faith (Mark 4:40), Jesus spoke to them sharply. On one occasion, however, the lack of understanding by the disciples seemed to provoke anger from Jesus as he directed these questions to them: "Do you still not perceive or understand? Are your hearts hardened? Do you have eyes, and fail to see? Do you have ears, and fail to hear? And do you not remember?" (Mark 8:17-18). Again, Jesus sounded angry when he spoke these words to Peter: "Get behind me, Satan! You are a stumbling block to me" (Matthew 16:23).

We do know that, if Jesus was angry on these or other occasions, he did not *stay* angry with his disciples. Quite the contrary, he patiently instructed them over and over again, accepting and loving them even when they failed. Why did forgiveness and acceptance follow Jesus' anger toward the disciples while a more negative attitude toward the religious leaders seemed to persist? Perhaps Jesus knew that the hearts of the disciples were open and that their intentions were good. The closed, hardened hearts of many of the religious leaders admitted neither error nor need for forgiveness.

Jesus did get angry, to be sure, but he tended his heart by dealing with his anger in healthy, appropriate ways. What do we see in his behavior that may be helpful to us? First of all, Jesus got angry about things worth getting angry about. For example, he was angry at the Pharisees when they preferred letting a person suffer rather than break Sabbath rules. He was angry with them for using their strict interpretation of Jewish law to tell persons they were unclean and unacceptable to God. Jesus' anger was usually against injustice and lack of mercy; against representing God in ways that did not show grace and love. Second, he always focused his anger on the specific issue or event at hand. He did not unleash his anger where it did not belong. Third, he expressed his anger immediately, clearly, and directly. He did not brood over whatever or whoever had made him angry.

How, then, do *we* keep our hearts from being eaten up with anger? First, we ask ourselves if the issue is worth the energy of anger. Frequently we may experience family members who are inattentive to us, coworkers who are not cooperative with us, friends whose bad habits irritate us, and strangers whose actions annoy us. Is expressing anger an appropriate response each time we are crossed? Perhaps many times we need to communicate our concerns without anger. While discerning which issues are worth getting angry about will not always be easy, we can be guided by Jesus who got angry about matters pertaining to God's justice, mercy, and love, as well as about persistent hardness of heart that prevented understanding his message. Talking with trusted family or friends and with God about what is making us angry will also guide us. If we think an issue warrants an angry response, then we should not hold it inside but, instead, direct it where it belongs.

We must carry the anger immediately to the appropriate person and express it in a healthy way—a way that does not cause physical, mental, or emotional harm to the other person or to ourselves. When events or circumstances are the cause of the anger, we must take whatever action is available to right the situation. And when we are up against a brick wall—such as the deaf ears and intolerance of the Pharisees—sometimes the best approach is to let out a deep sigh and walk away.

"No More of This!"

While he was still speaking, suddenly a crowd came, and the one called Judas, one of the twelve, was leading them. He approached Jesus to kiss him; but Jesus said to him, "Judas, is it with a kiss that you are betraying the Son of Man?" When those who were around him saw what was coming, they asked, "Lord, should we strike with the sword?" Then one of them struck the slave of the high priest and cut off his right ear. But Jesus said, "No more of this!" And he touched his ear and healed him. (Luke 22:47-51)

This hour, and the hours that followed, were filled with anger. We see anger from the disciples. The Gospel of John reports that Peter was the one who cut off the ear of the high priest's slave (18:10). Peter's temper flared, and he acted impulsively as he had done several times in the past. He was angry. Perhaps he had been angry since earlier in the evening. Then, Jesus said to Peter, "You will deny me three times" (Mark 14:30). Peter was defensive, perhaps even angered by the accusation. He said he would never deny Jesus. Later in the evening, Peter was certainly angry when questioned repeatedly about his association with Jesus. At the third denial, Peter "began to curse, and he swore an oath" (Matthew 26:74).

Judas, the disciple who betrayed Jesus, may have acted partly out of anger that Jesus had refused to be the Messiah that Judas wanted him to be. Perhaps other disciples were angered by the hostile action of the religious leaders and the opposition from the fickle crowd.

But Jesus said, "No more of this!" (Luke 22:51).

The crowd involved in the events of these hours was angry, too. They came with Judas carrying swords and clubs. Perhaps their anger was fueled by their own impatience that this teacher had not relieved their suffering and oppression under Roman rule. Certainly their anger had been fueled by the false accusations of the religious leaders. Soon the crowd would be yelling, "Crucify him!"

But Jesus said, "No more of this!"

The religious leaders had been angry with Jesus almost from the beginning. Jesus had not followed the rules to which they had devoted their lives, and he had told them on more than one occasion that they were wrong. That Jesus had attracted a large crowd did not help matters. Later, the high priest, after talking briefly with Jesus, displayed considerable anger. He "tore his clothes and said, 'He has blasphemed! Why do we still need witnesses?' " (Matthew 26:65). The scribes and elders gathered around the high priest were angry, too. We read, "Then they spat in [Jesus'] face and struck him; and some slapped him" (Matthew 26:67).

But Jesus said, "No more of this!"

Was Jesus angry, too? Were these four words, "No more of this!" yelled in anger? Certainly Jesus had good reason to be angry at Judas for betraying him. Perhaps he was angry at Peter for acting violently. The crowd might have included many who had followed Jesus and had heard him teach—some who might have witnessed the healing of a friend or family member—and now they had turned on him. Didn't he have cause to be angry? And how could Jesus not be angry at the priests and other religious leaders who had schemed and plotted to have him arrested? He had been angry at them many times before. In other words, Jesus was in a situation full of things worth getting angry about.

Look, however, at the words Jesus spoke immediately before and after his arrest. His words do not sound angry. When confronted by Judas, Jesus said to him, "Friend, do what you are here to do" (Matthew 26:50). To Peter, Jesus said, "Put your sword back into its place; for all who take the sword will perish by the sword" (Matthew 26:52). Before Caiaphas the high priest, Jesus was silent until pushed to respond. When he did speak, his words did not suggest anger.

"No more of this!" What is *this* to which Jesus referred? Perhaps he was saying, "No more anger." The anger expressed around him arose from different persons and groups and for different reasons, but none of it was healthy. The leaders of his faith tradition, the crowd of followers, and even his own disciples had failed to understand his ministry, the gospel he had preached. Jesus had made his decision. He would let the religious leaders think they had won. He would let the crowd have their way. He would let the disciples off the hook, allowing them to run.

The situation has similarities to a divided church where factions have resorted to recruiting people for their side, holding secret meetings, manipulating, and being deceitful. Presentation of logical arguments has ended. No one is still listening to the other side. Almost everyone is angry. Finally, the ones who have tried to remain in the middle to mediate a compromise have given up. The anger has become too destructive. It is time to close this door and move on. "No more of this."

Jesus tended his heart, even his whole being, at this stage in his ministry. He let go of anger and accepted defeat—granted, only a temporary defeat, because others had not accepted what he had preached, but a defeat nevertheless. His response went beyond what he had done in the past when he had let out a sigh and walked away. Those times he had known he would return to argue with the Pharisees another day and perhaps get angry again. This time, he knew his decision was more final than before.

Why would Jesus let go of his anger and resign himself to the consequences? Perhaps he was acting in response to his calling to follow a more sacrificial path as suggested in the gospel accounts (e.g., Matthew 20:18-19). Perhaps he also saw the violence—the fighting and death of others—that might result if he allowed any acts of resistance. How could the peacemaker allow himself or his disciples to fight in anger for his ministry of love? Nevertheless, as disciples, religious leaders, and others in the crowd displayed their anger, surely Jesus must have felt pain, sharp and deep, as he refused to fight back, as he accepted whatever would come. Tending body, heart, mind, and soul—even the best kind of tending—cannot always prevent pain.

We may face a situation when we know we are right and our opponents are wrong. We may know, too, that continuing to fight to win may result in a loss of some kind—perhaps the loss of who we know ourselves to be. How can we possibly choose to accept defeat? May we hear the words of Jesus once again as we "look" at his face, gazing into his eyes. May we listen carefully to his resignation as he says, "No more of this!"

Grief

Grief is a powerful emotion. It is often deeply and painfully felt, sometimes overwhelming not only the heart but also the body, mind, and soul. Grief may be so long-lasting and pervasive that it is destructive, totally debilitating the person experiencing it. Jesus knew grief. He experienced the death of persons to whom he felt close. He grieved over the Jews in Jerusalem and perhaps others who did not understand or would not accept God's intentions and God's love for them. Also, toward the end of his life, Jesus experienced grief over his own life, particularly what he was facing. How did he deal with his grief so that it did not consume him? Consider these three examples of how Jesus tended his heart by dealing with his grief.

Herod had John the Baptist beheaded as requested by the young girl who had danced for him at his party (Matthew 14:1-12). Although the text says that "the king was grieved" to keep his thoughtless promise to grant the girl's request, surely he did not truly grieve over this death. The real grief was borne by John the Baptist's disciples and others who loved him, including Jesus.

Jesus' mother, Mary, and John's mother, Elizabeth, were cousins and friends. We know that Mary visited Elizabeth while each was pregnant. Perhaps after the births of their sons, the women met and let their boys play together. When they were young men, Jesus and John met again. John the Baptist was already pursuing his call to preach repentance when Jesus came to him to be baptized. Jesus soon began his own ministry. Perhaps the two met after that. Several gospel texts suggest each was aware of the ministry of the other (e.g., Luke 7:18-34). When Jesus was told about John's death, surely he was deeply grieved. We read, "Now when Jesus heard this, he withdrew from there in a boat to a deserted place by himself" (Matthew 14:13). Jesus' first response to this terrible news was to escape from everyone to be alone. However, the crowds followed him. Jesus responded to their needs, healing the sick and providing fish and bread for thousands of them to eat. A second time, however, he sent the disciples ahead by boat and he dismissed the crowds. Then, "he went up the mountain by himself to pray" (Matthew 14:23). Jesus tended his grieving heart by being alone with his own thoughts, memories, and pain, and by being with God, intentionally and quietly.

Jesus needed time alone to grieve. He did not, however, stay away for long, isolating himself and losing himself in his grief. After the night alone in prayer and reflection, he returned to his disciples early the next morning. Certainly the story of the reunion is dramatic as Jesus walked on the water toward the boat on which the disciples had spent the night (Matthew 14:25). Reunited with his disciples, Jesus immediately returned to work. As soon as they arrived at Gennesaret, Jesus resumed his healing ministry.

Another death of someone to whom Jesus was very close also caused him deep grief. Jesus' friend Lazarus, the brother of his close friends Mary and Martha, died. Jesus delayed going to Bethany where these friends lived. When he arrived a few days after Lazarus's death, he was met first by Martha and later by Mary. Mary knelt at Jesus' feet and said that her brother would not have died had Jesus been there. "When Jesus saw her weeping, and the Jews who came with her also weeping, he was greatly disturbed in spirit and deeply moved" (John 11:33). Picture this scene; feel the emotion. The description of Jesus' response makes clear the depth of his grief. He was "greatly disturbed" and "deeply moved." How did Jesus tend the emotional upheaval he felt at that moment? "Jesus began to weep" (John 11:35). Jesus released emotion in his tears, joining with the other mourners who were crying for Lazarus. The response helped tend his heart. The writer of the Gospel of John describes how Jesus then took away the grief—his own and that of all the others gathered—by calling Lazarus out from his grave.

A third example of how Jesus dealt with grief came during the final days of his life. After the Passover meal, Jesus took his disciples with him to Gethsemane. "He took with him Peter and the two sons of Zebedee, and began to be grieved and agitated. Then he said to them, 'I am deeply grieved, even to death; remain here, and stay awake with me'" (Matthew 26:37-38). Jesus was grieving. The Gospels suggest many reasons for his grief. Instead of embracing the good news about the kingdom of God that he had preached, the Jewish leaders had rejected him—in fact, they actively had opposed him. Jesus was in Jerusalem. He knew that his ministry and perhaps his life were at considerable risk. Soon, Judas would betray him. Other reasons for grief awaited him. He would be arrested. His closest companions would desert him. He would be tried, convicted, and killed.

How did Jesus tend his grief in this dark hour in the garden before the darker hours ahead? First, he talked honestly with his best friends, acknowledging to them his deep grief and asking for their presence in praying with him. Second, he talked honestly with God. Three times he prayed, "My Father, if it is possible, let this cup pass from me; yet not what I want but what you want" (Matthew 26:39). What we hear is blunt honesty: "God, don't make me do this." Finally, however, Jesus moves on to face what he must face. He does so with strength and grace. After waking his sleeping disciples for a third time, he says to them, "Get up, let us be going. See, my betrayer is at hand" (Matthew 26:46).

Jesus encountered grief many times during the brief period for which we have recorded accounts. These three experiences—John the Baptist's beheading, Lazarus's death, and his own agony during his final days—may have been the most difficult, but surely they were not the only causes of grief. Through them all, Jesus tended his heart well in his grief.

How can Jesus' example guide us in our own grief? Jesus teaches us to spend time alone, particularly time alone with God, and to return to friends and family to resume the lives we have been called to live. When our grief is overwhelming, we can release it in tears as Jesus did—both privately and in community with others who mourn. We also must talk honestly about our grief, seeking support from close friends and courage and strength from God. Finally, we can face the cup we must face knowing that Jesus has suffered before us and God is suffering with us.

"Shake Off the Dust"

He left that place and came to his hometown, and his disciples fol-lowed him. On the sabbath he began to teach in the synagogue, and many who heard him were astounded. They said, "Where did this man get all this? What is this wisdom that has been given to him? What deeds of power are being done by his hands! Is not this the car-penter, the son of Mary and brother of James and Joses and Judas and Simon, and are not his sisters here with us?" And they took offense at him. Then Jesus said to them, "Prophets are not without honor, except in their hometown, and among their own kin, and in

*their own house." And he could do no deed of power there, except
that he laid his hands on a few sick people and cured them. And he
was amazed at their unbelief.*

*Then he went about among the villages teaching. He called the
twelve and began to send them out two by two, and gave them
authority over the unclean spirits. He ordered them to take nothing
for their journey except a staff; no bread, no bag, no money in their
belts; but to wear sandals and not to put on two tunics. He said to
them, "Wherever you enter a house, stay there until you leave the
place. If any place will not welcome you and they refuse to hear you,
as you leave, shake off the dust that is on your feet as a testimony
against them." So they went out and proclaimed that all should
repent. They cast out many demons, and anointed with oil many
who were sick and cured them. (Mark 6:1-13)*

Jesus arrived in his hometown to teach, preach, and heal as he had
been doing in other towns. A parallel account in the Gospel of Luke
indicates that Nazareth was the "hometown" where family, friends, and
neighbors were questioning Jesus' authority (4:16-30). In the second
part of the passage from the Gospel of Mark, Jesus called his disciples
together to instruct them and to send them out as missionaries. He sent
them out in pairs and told them to travel light, advising them about
how to respond when they were not well received. "Shake off the dust
that is on your feet," he told them (v. 11). Jesus was always a model for
the adage "practice what you preach." The experience in Nazareth was
the "practicing" while the instruction to the disciples was the "preaching." Jesus had been rejected, but he had responded by moving on. He
was telling his disciples to do the same. One lesson we can learn from
Jesus' actions and words is this: There is a time *not* to grieve.

Grief is a deeply felt, usually extremely painful emotional response to
a loss. Jesus grieved over the deaths of John the Baptist and Lazarus. He
grieved in the garden of Gethsemane over his own life, particularly the
path that lay before him. In this text and others, however, Jesus' example suggests that not every loss is good cause for grief. In particular,
rejection—of our message or advice, of the product we are offering, or
even of ourselves—is not always an appropriate occasion for grief.

Most people experience rejection at some point in their lives. A girl
may be rejected by her high school boyfriend. A guy may be rejected by

the college that was first on his list. A woman may not get the expected job offer from the major accounting firm. A father's advice may be rejected by his son who then makes bad, even dangerous, choices. A preacher's stewardship appeal may be rejected by the congregation. The list goes on and on. How do we respond to rejection?

When rejected, we cannot prevent an immediate response of sorrow or even pangs of grief. Still, do we tend our hearts by embracing the grief or by shaking off the grief and moving on more quickly than a full experience of grief would allow? In numerous cases of obvious loss or rejection, Jesus moved on quickly to the next task with no mention in the text of taking time to tend a grieving heart. Certainly we do not find clear, specific rules for when to grieve and when not to grieve. Sometimes rejection, perhaps by a spouse who wants a divorce, is a cause for deep grief. Tending one's heart following a loss of any kind is sensitive and subjective territory. Looking at Jesus, however, we do find examples to prepare and encourage us when it is time to let go of rejection and move on.

When Jesus told the rich, young ruler to sell everything that he had, the man rejected the call and went away grieving. Although the account in Mark 10:17-22 tells us that Jesus had looked at the man and "loved him," Jesus did not stop to grieve this man's walking away. Instead he used the occasion to teach about the problem of riches. On another occasion, Jesus healed ten lepers, yet only one returned to thank him (Luke 17:11-19). Although the other nine did not specifically reject Jesus, they failed to appreciate the life-changing, life-giving healing of Jesus. Jesus did not get angry or grieve over being taken for granted. Instead, he affirmed the one who returned, saying, "Get up and go on your way; your faith has made you well" (Luke 17:19).

These examples are minor, however, in comparison to the rejection Jesus experienced in Nazareth. People who knew Jesus—friends with whom he had grown up—rejected him. They "took offense" at him (Mark 6:3). Jesus' words about prophets not being honored "among their own kin" (v. 4) suggest that members of his own family rejected him as well. The parallel account in Luke indicates the degree of rejection. The hometown folks listening to Jesus in the synagogue "got up, drove [Jesus] out of the town, and led him to the brow of the hill on which their town was built, so that they might hurl him off the cliff"

(Luke 4:29). This is serious rejection which, for many of us, would certainly cause considerable grief. As we read in Mark's account, however, Jesus' response was to go "about among the villages teaching" (6:6).

Jesus expected his disciples to follow his example. They were not to expect success in all their missionary efforts. He did not want them to brood and grieve over their "failure" when rejected. Neither did he tell them to never give up and to try, try, try again. Rather, Jesus said, "Shake off the dust." In other words, when rejected, let it go and move on.

The writer of Ecclesiastes says that there is "a time to mourn, and a time to dance" (3:4b). This is true, but this is not the whole truth. In between mourning and dancing is another time—a time *not* to mourn. This time is not for celebration and dancing. It is perhaps best described by the phrase from Isaiah 40:31 as a time to "walk and not faint." Jesus tended his heart by grieving over some losses and not grieving over others. He shows us that sometimes rejection, even painful rejection, is a time *not* to grieve.

When faced with a loss, may Jesus' example help guide the tending of our hearts. Perhaps it is time to shake off the dust and move on.

Compassion

Jesus cared deeply about the well-being of others. He identified with and felt sympathy for those who were hurting. He was compassionate. Jesus tended his heart not merely by *feeling* compassion but by *showing* compassion. His compassion for the sick, the blind, the hungry, the grieving, and the vulnerable resulted in action to help alleviate their suffering. "When [Jesus] saw the crowds, he had compassion for them, because they were harassed and helpless, like sheep without a shepherd" (Matthew 9:36). Jesus' actions empowered people, moving them out of helplessness toward wholeness.

Jesus' compassion was revealed clearly and frequently as he healed people who were sick, blind, or disabled. The man with leprosy was excluded from the community because of his disease (Luke 5:12-14). When Jesus made him clean, he could reenter society. Similarly, the blind men crying out to Jesus from the side of the road were also excluded from participation in society (Matthew 20:29-34). Some Jews thought sin caused blindness and other illnesses and disabilities. They believed that such sinfulness made these men unclean. But Jesus was "moved with compassion" and "touched their eyes" so that they regained their sight. Now they could be productive and "acceptable" members of the community. They chose to follow Jesus. On another occasion, in the country of the Gerasenes, Jesus encountered a man possessed by demons—a man clearly ostracized by his community (Luke 8:26-39). When Jesus rid the man of his demons, this man also wanted to follow Jesus. But Jesus told him to be a missionary in his own town. In all these cases and in many others, Jesus' compassionate healing restored physical health and removed barriers that excluded individuals from the community.

On one particular occasion, Jesus showed compassion toward a large crowd that had followed him when he and the disciples were trying to get away to rest (Mark 6:30-44). Responding to the crowd, Jesus taught throughout the day. Later, the compassion of the disciples was evident as they expressed concern that the people were growing hungry. They said to Jesus, "This is a deserted place, and the hour is now very late; send them away so that they may go into the surrounding country and villages and buy something for themselves to eat" (Mark 6:35-36). Jesus' compassion, however, caused him to assume responsibility to meet the needs of the people immediately. The people were hungry. Jesus fed them. No questions. No red tape. Jesus prepared a meal for thousands.

Jesus also showed compassion for people who were vulnerable, who had no status in society. Among these powerless people were women. When Jesus saw the widow from Nain, whose only son had died, "he had compassion for her and said to her, 'Do not weep' " (Luke 7:13). Then he brought the young man back to life. On another occasion, Jesus defended the woman who had washed his feet and anointed them with oil (Luke 7:36-50). She was called a sinner and considered unclean—someone a "real" prophet, according to the Pharisees, would not allow to touch him. Yet Jesus offered her acceptance and forgiveness, telling her to "go in peace." Even the disciples were shocked when Jesus was talking to another "sinful" woman, the woman at the well in Samaria (John 4:7-30). Jesus showed compassion toward her by speaking to her, listening to her, and treating her with respect. Yet another woman, this one in grave danger because she was accused of adultery, was brought to Jesus (John 8:3-11). Again, out of compassion, he defended the vulnerable woman, defeating her accusers with his wisdom and sending her on her way. In each case, Jesus showed compassion in championing the cause of the vulnerable one.

Jesus acknowledged and valued not only women, but also children. He showed compassion for these young ones who did not count in the society. Even the disciples did not offer compassion to the ones trying to bring their children to Jesus. But Jesus said, "Let the little children come to me, and do not stop them; for it is to such as these that the kingdom of God belongs" (Luke 18:16). Jesus held these little ones in his arms and blessed them.

As we have seen, Jesus demonstrated compassion in many ways. First, with no discomfort or hesitation, he did everything he could to enable those with physical difficulties—the sick, blind, diseased, and lame—to be restored to wholeness. By doing so, he removed barriers to their being part of the community. Though we cannot heal as Jesus did, we can go beyond merely feeling compassion. For example, we can be advocates for those who need help in obtaining health care. We can be patient, welcoming, and supportive of those whose physical limitations make them different.

Second, Jesus acted to meet needs. People were hungry, so he fed them. He did not rebuke them for their lack of responsibility in showing up without adequate provisions. Nor did he follow the disciples' suggestion to send everyone off to find their own food. We, too, can respond immediately at times to meet a basic need—such as food, clothing, or shelter.

Third, Jesus acted to affirm the worth of women, children, and other excluded persons and to include them in the community. In word and action, Jesus communicated to vulnerable and marginalized persons, as well as to those rejecting them, that each is a person of value deserving respect and care. Certainly we are called to follow his example in acts of kindness and inclusion to those demeaned, rejected, or unfairly labeled by society as "sinful."

Jesus felt compassion toward hurting people. Being a compassionate person, however, did not mean merely feeling sympathy and talking about the feeling. For Jesus, compassion meant action. He teaches us that true compassion always reaches out to help.

"Filled with Compassion; He Ran"

Then Jesus said, "There was a man who had two sons. The younger of them said to his father, 'Father, give me the share of the property that will belong to me.' So he divided his property between them. A few days later the younger son gathered all he had and traveled to a distant country, and there he squandered his property in dissolute living. When he had spent everything, a severe famine took place throughout that country, and he began to be in need. So he went and hired himself out to one of the citizens of that country, who sent him to his fields to feed the pigs. He would gladly have filled himself with the pods that the pigs were eating; and no one gave him anything. But when he came to himself he said, 'How many of my father's hired hands have bread enough and to spare, but here I am dying of hunger! I will get up and go to my father, and I will say to him, "Father, I have sinned against heaven and before you; I am no longer worthy to be called your son; treat me like one of your hired hands."' So he set off and went to his father. But while he was still far off, his father saw him and was filled with compassion; he ran and put his arms around him and kissed him. Then the son said to him, 'Father, I have sinned against heaven and before you; I am no longer worthy to be called your son.' But the father said to his slaves, 'Quickly, bring out a robe—the best one—and put it on him; put a ring on his finger and sandals on his feet. And get the fatted calf and kill it, and let us eat and celebrate; for this son of mine was dead and is alive again; he was lost and is found!' And they began to celebrate.

"Now his elder son was in the field; and when he came and approached the house, he heard music and dancing. He called one of the slaves and asked what was going on. He replied, 'Your brother has come, and your father has killed the fatted calf, because he has got him back safe and sound.' Then he became angry and refused to go in. His father came out and began to plead with him. But he answered his father, 'Listen! For all these years I have been working like a slave for you, and I have never disobeyed your command; yet you have never given me even a young goat so that I might celebrate with my friends. But when this son of yours came back, who has devoured your property with prostitutes, you killed the fatted calf for him!' Then the father said to him, 'Son, you are always with me, and all that is mine is yours. But we had to celebrate and rejoice, because

this brother of yours was dead and has come to life; he was lost and has been found.'" (Luke 15:11-32)

This story, familiar to many as the parable of the Prodigal Son, is one of several lost-and-found parables told by Jesus. A group of "tax collectors and sinners" were listening to Jesus when "Pharisees and scribes" arrived and criticized Jesus for associating with sinners (Luke 15:1-2). Jesus told three parables in response to the religious leaders' criticism. In each of these parables, the one finding what had been lost—a sheep, a coin, or a son—rejoiced and celebrated. Jesus was teaching about God's concern, care, and love for everyone who is lost. This parable of the father and his sons is not only a lost-and-found story revealing God's love, but also a story rich with emotions of the heart.

Each son is an example of what can happen when emotions of the heart are not tended well. The younger son is restless, ambitious, ungrateful, and greedy. Perhaps he feels that his life would be much better were he free of family restrictions, responsibilities, and expecta-tions—free to chase after riches and women. The young man disre-spectfully asks his father for his share of the property. Upon receiving it, he takes off impulsively, thoughtlessly trying to satisfy the desires of his heart. Soon, the rush to satisfy dissolves into distress and despair. He is miserable and hungry.

One lesson we can learn at this point from the younger son's exam-ple is the danger of allowing the desires of the heart to have free rein. Tending the heart is not accomplished by unfettered expression of any and every desire. Eventually the young man pauses to reflect, perhaps with some guilt, on what he has done in squandering his inheritance. Perhaps he feels deep sorrow and regret over taking his property and leaving his father. All we know for sure, however, is that the young man realizes that going back to his father is better than starvation.

The older son's reaction to his brother's return reveals an unhealthy heart as well. His problem is the opposite of his brother's. While the younger son acted on his emotions without much thought, the older son brooded over events and held on to his negative emotions. On learning of the celebration of his brother's return, the older son responds immediately with an outburst of venom. He has nurtured anger in his heart, along with resentment toward his brother. He likely has kept a mental list of all the things he has done to deserve reward and all the things his father has not done to show appreciation. He has stored in his mind evidence against his family, which has hardened his heart. So, when his brother returns, the older son is enraged at the inequity in the treatment the young man receives relative to what he deserves.

Between these two unhealthy hearts is the heart of the father, filled with compassion. In this story that Jesus tells, as in Jesus' own life, we see that tending a heart full of compassion requires action. When he saw his young son in the distance, the father "ran and put his arms around him and kissed him" (15:20). No questions asked. He gave the son gifts and called for a feast, reaching out with forgiveness even before hearing repentance from his son. Immediately he offered love to the one who had previously rejected him. The father showed compassion for his older son, too, by going out to him and pleading with him to join the celebration—an action that was unexpected and not required.

The lesson here may be difficult for us to accept. The father has two ungrateful sons, yet he responds to their ingratitude with compassionate acts of love offered again and again—no matter what. Remember, Jesus was making a point to the scribes and Pharisees who criticized him for "welcoming sinners." Those religious leaders did not have compassion for the lost ones among them.

In the lost-and-found stories in Luke 15, Jesus identified the lost not only as a vulnerable lamb, but also as a privileged young man who makes bad choices, and another privileged young man with a bad attitude. Jesus' examples teach us that compassion is not only for those we know and like and think deserve our sympathy. Jesus had compassion on all those who were hurting, vulnerable, and powerless. He also had compassion on those who were powerful but who needed forgiveness and acceptance. We may tend our own hearts by seeing others through the eyes of Jesus—by showing the same compassion as the father showed his wayward son and his resentful son. Are we, like the father, "filled with compassion"? If so, we should be running out to meet and embrace all our brothers and sisters, our sons and daughters, who have lost their way.

Passion

The word *passion* and the name *Jesus* are usually combined only to describe the suffering of Jesus during the last week of his life. Apart from such references, *passion* may not often be applied to Jesus because the word is frequently associated with sexual desire—not a frequent subject for sermons about Jesus, to say the least! Passion, however, has other meanings. It can refer, for example, to one's deep commitment to a cause, or to one's enthusiasm for and devotion to a vocation. Jesus had a heart full of passion. His teaching, preaching, and actions all revealed his heartfelt passion for proclaiming the good news of the kingdom of God, for doing justice, and for showing mercy. Throughout his ministry, Jesus tended his heart by working out his passions in positive ways. He talked about the kingdom of God to anyone who would listen. In all of his living, he revealed who God is. Jesus demonstrated justice and mercy toward all people, particularly those who were weak and vulnerable, and he challenged and called others to follow his example.

After his forty days of testing in the wilderness, Jesus soon returned to Nazareth where he went to the synagogue to teach. Opening a scroll of Isaiah, Jesus read as follows: "The Spirit of the Lord is upon me, / because he has anointed me / to bring good news to the poor. / He has sent me to proclaim release to the captives / and recovery of sight to the blind, / to let the oppressed go free, / to proclaim the year of the Lord's favor" (Luke 4:16-19). The prophet Isaiah's words speak of good news and of justice and of mercy. Jesus acknowledged that he was the fulfillment of this prophecy (Luke 4:21). He understood his mission and was passionate about pursuing it.

Jesus was passionate in his preaching about the good news of the kingdom of God. He told his listeners to "strive first for the kingdom of God" (Matthew 6:33). As we read the Synoptic Gospels, we discover how often Jesus taught and preached about the kingdom. In a statement summarizing Jesus' ministry, we read that "Jesus went about all the cities and villages, teaching in their synagogues, and proclaiming the good news of the kingdom, and curing every disease and every sickness" (Matthew 9:35). When sending out his disciples to do missionary work, Jesus defined their mission similarly. We read in the Gospel of Luke: "Jesus called the twelve together and gave them power and authority over all demons and to cure diseases, and he sent them out to proclaim the kingdom of God and to heal" (9:1-2).

In addition to preaching directly the good news of the kingdom, Jesus told numerous parables to illustrate and explain the kingdom of God. He described the kingdom using rich and varied images—a mustard seed, a treasure hidden in a field, a priceless pearl, and others. His frequent, poetic, and picturesque references reveal his unmistakable passion for the kingdom of God.

How did Jesus tend his heart given his passion for the kingdom of God? Most obviously, Jesus found a way to express his passion—he preached it and taught it. This was his theme. In fact, we could say that all of his teaching and preaching was related to his basic message about the kingdom of God. He preached to religious leaders, who argued with him and became angry. He taught his disciples, who often did not understand him. He preached to everyone who would listen. Jesus was persistent and determined, often preaching his message in the face of disappointment and opposition. He also was creative in expressing his passion, continually using new examples and images to communicate his message. Jesus tried to convince others to believe what he taught and to live as he lived, but he never compromised his passion in order to make his message and himself more acceptable. Surely his heart was troubled by the rejection of his message by so many people, yet he refused to stifle or reject his own passion for what he knew to be true, for what he knew mattered most.

Jesus' passion for doing justice and showing mercy flowed from his passion about the kingdom of God—for God is just and merciful. Although Jesus did not want to overturn Jewish law, he did want to overturn the way the law was interpreted and enforced by religious leaders. He accused the Pharisees and others of imposing the law in ways that promoted injustices and lacked mercy. On numerous occasions, he challenged the Pharisees in their interpretation of Sabbath laws. For example, Jesus showed mercy by healing on the Sabbath (e.g., Mark 3:1-5) and by allowing the disciples to pluck grain to eat on the Sabbath (Mark 2:23-28). Jesus also challenged the laws regarding what is clean and what is unclean by not washing in the required manner before eating a meal (Luke 11:37-41). His words to the religious leaders on these matters of the law were harsh: "Woe to you, scribes and Pharisees, hypocrites! For you tithe mint, dill, and cummin, and have neglected the weightier matters of the law: justice and mercy and faith" (Matthew 23:23).

Jesus tended his heart well by actively challenging the injustice of the religious leaders. He decried the injustice of using the law to ostracize people who had been labeled unclean and to refuse help to people in need. Jesus showed the law to be merciful. He dined with "unclean" sinners; welcomed children; healed the sick, blind, and lame; and protected those judged wrongly. The Pharisees, on the other hand, directed their passion for the law in negative ways. They used their energy to find fault in others and exclude them from the religious community. They passionately opposed Jesus, using the law to trap him. What perhaps was once a righteous passion for the law had become an unrighteous passion against those who did not keep the law according to the Pharisees' standards. Jesus said that their hearts were hardened—which often happens when passion is directed *against* some*one* instead of *for* some*thing*.

Jesus was a rebel. He had a fiery passion for the kingdom of God, a kingdom of justice, mercy, and love. He preached it. He taught it. He acted and fought on behalf of it. Although the religious leaders did not accept his interpretation of Sabbath and cleanliness laws, or his good news about the kingdom of God, Jesus remained devoted to his cause. To the end, he was a man with a heart full of passion, and he tended his heart well.

"He Called Her Over"

Now he was teaching in one of the synagogues on the sabbath. And just then there appeared a woman with a spirit that had crippled her for eighteen years. She was bent over and was quite unable to stand up straight. When Jesus saw her, he called her over and said, "Woman, you are set free from your ailment." When he laid his hands on her, immediately she stood up straight and began praising God. But the leader of the synagogue, indignant because Jesus had cured on the sabbath, kept saying to the crowd, "There are six days on which work ought to be done; come on those days and be cured, and not on the sabbath day." But the Lord answered him and said, "You hypocrites! Does not each of you on the sabbath untie his ox or his donkey from the manger, and lead it away to give it water? And ought not this woman, a daughter of Abraham whom Satan bound for eighteen long years, be set free from this bondage on the sabbath day?" When he said this, all his opponents were put to shame; and the entire crowd was rejoicing at all the wonderful things that he was doing. (Luke 13:10-17)

Throughout his ministry, Jesus had compassion for people who were sick, disabled, or suffering from mental illness. People shouted to Jesus, asking him for help. Friends and family brought loved ones to Jesus to be healed. Some people fell at Jesus' feet asking for help. Jesus demonstrated compassion in healing the ones who came or were brought to him. This passage shows Jesus' compassion for the woman who had suffered for eighteen years, but the details reveal something more.

Jesus was teaching in the synagogue on the Sabbath, as was his custom. The text says that a woman appeared. No mention is made, however, of any action on her part to encounter Jesus and to ask for help. She did not call to him or go over to him or ask anything of him at any point. The woman is described as being "bent over and . . . quite unable to stand up straight" (Luke 13:11). Picture this woman as she came into the synagogue. She was so stooped that her face was parallel to the ground. She looked downward and probably did not see Jesus. Of course, we cannot know. Perhaps she had heard that the Healer was there, and she had come hoping to see him. Nevertheless, the text records only that Jesus called to her and asked her to come to him.

Jesus did not need to recruit people who needed healing. His reputation as a powerful healer was established. He demonstrated his compassion for hours, for days, in many towns and villages as people flocked to him. At times he had to leave with people still waiting to be healed. Why did he take the initiative with this particular woman? Surely upon seeing her he had compassion for her in her suffering. Perhaps he was motivated, as well, to make a point about his passion for justice and for mercy regardless of Sabbath laws.

Jesus knew his audience. The leader of the synagogue was watching. Surely Jesus could have spoken quietly to the woman, asking her to meet him the next day or suggesting she come to a healing service later in the week. Instead, he acted immediately, demonstrating his belief that the Sabbath laws were burdensome and unfair. Although Jesus certainly showed compassion for the crippled woman, this healing seems to have an "in your face" tone to it. We might imagine Jesus thinking, "Are you religious leaders watching what I'm going to do?" As soon as Jesus healed the woman, the leader of the synagogue protested, not so much to Jesus as to the crowd. Having provoked a confrontation by healing on the Sabbath, Jesus accepted the challenge and fired back his own charges.

Some of the civil rights actions in this country during the 1950s and 1960s are reminiscent of Jesus' act of protest. Rosa Parks may have needed transportation from one place to another, but the act of refusing to give up her seat on the bus was an act of protest. The four black college students who sat at the lunch counter at Woolworth's in Greensboro, North Carolina, may have been hungry and may have wanted to order lunch. However, they were aware of the law and of who was watching. Where they chose to eat was a deliberate act of protest. The civil rights activists were full of passion for justice. This healing act by Jesus is similar to those more recent acts of protest. Jesus saw a chance to make a dramatic point about justice and mercy. The religious leaders were "put to shame," and the crowd rejoiced.

Expressing one's passion is not by invitation only. A musician plays his violin in the same place in the park or in front of the same store day after day, not only unpaid but also uninvited. A church member makes a plea every Sunday for more volunteers to visit the homebound members. A citizen requests time at every school board meeting to ask for more opportunities for gifted students or for students with disabilities. Likewise, in exercising his passion for what he believed in, Jesus was persistent and aggressive. The risk to his ministry and personal safely increased with every day that he challenged the religious leaders, yet he did not back off.

The gospel writers did not have to guess what was really important to Jesus. He tended his heart by living his life and doing his ministry out of his passion. When looking at Jesus' passion—for the kingdom of God and for justice and mercy—we are reminded of the slogan made famous by Nike: "Just do it." Jesus did—always.

Priorities

Jesus said, "For where your treasure is, there your heart will be also" (Matthew 6:21). This verse is part of a brief passage in the Sermon on the Mount in which Jesus said we are to store up treasure in heaven rather than on earth. Our heart, he explained, moves to and resides with our treasure. Our "treasure" is what we value most, our priority in life. Our priority is determined not by what we say but by how we live. It is whatever we are attached to in such a way that we cannot imagine letting go. Our treasure, then, may be a thing, an activity, an attitude, a person, or a habit. The condition of our hearts is dependent on what we treasure. If our priority is something that is destructive or that does not satisfy, we will have a troubled and unhealthy heart.

Jesus' priority was his relationship with God. He lived in harmony with God and in accordance with God's requirement "to do justice, and to love kindness, and to walk humbly with . . . God" (Micah 6:8). During his life, he followed a path in keeping with God's will. He tended his heart by not letting any other priority come between himself and God. Being well aware of the earthly treasures that tempt women and men, Jesus preached against these often. Frequently he challenged persons he encountered to look honestly at themselves and to consider what they treasured.

The most common and most dangerous "treasure," and the attachment Jesus preached against most often, is wealth. Recognizing that being rich can easily become a stumbling block in one's relationship with God, Jesus preached that "you cannot serve God and wealth" (Matthew 6:24). He warned that "it is easier for a camel to go through the eye of a needle than for someone who is rich to enter the kingdom of God" (Luke 18:25). To impress on his listeners the danger of making wealth a priority, Jesus told parables. After the rich fool built more barns to hold his excess crops, God told him that his life would be taken that night. Jesus concluded the story, saying, "So it is with those who store up treasures for themselves but are not rich toward God" (Luke 12:21).

In one of the best-known confrontations about priorities in the Gospels, Jesus told the rich ruler, who seemed proud of how he had kept the law, to "sell all that you own and distribute the money to the poor, and you will have treasure in heaven; then come, follow me" (Luke 18:22). The ruler refused because he was very rich. Jesus did not say that having wealth and making God top priority were absolutely incompatible. In fact, it is likely that women who provided for Jesus and friends who gave dinner parties and feasts in his honor had above-average means. Joseph of Arimathea, a disciple of Jesus, is even described as rich. Nevertheless, Jesus was clear about the difficulty of rich people being devoted to God.

The danger of being attached to power, authority, and position was another warning of Jesus. He frequently criticized the Pharisees for the arrogant ways they used their authority to accuse others of not following the law, to exclude Jews from the religious community, and to proclaim non-Jews outside of God's acceptance and love. Among many stinging charges, Jesus said of the scribes and Pharisees: "They tie up heavy burdens, hard to bear, and lay them on the shoulders of others. . . . They do all their deeds to be seen by others. . . . They love to have the place of honor at banquets. . . . [They love] to be greeted with respect in the marketplaces" (Matthew 23:4-7). How heartbreaking the Pharisees' corruption of the religious community and system must have been for Jesus. The very ones who claimed to have God as their treasure were hypocrites who "on the outside look[ed] righteous to others, but inside . . . [were] full of hypocrisy and lawlessness" (Matthew 23:28).

Jesus did not say that having authority and power precluded having a heart devoted to God. The centurion asking Jesus to heal his servant acknowledged his own authority yet humbled himself before Jesus, and Jesus commended the man's faith (Matthew 8:5-13). Yet when his own disciples, James and John, asked for places of power in Jesus' kingdom, Jesus questioned their understanding of what they were asking of him (Mark 10:35-40). Even these close friends and followers had their eyes on greatness. Jesus reminded them that his call, for himself and for every follower, was to be a servant.

In addition to wealth and power or position, Jesus noted other priorities that can draw the heart away from God. Some attachments he questioned may make us very uncomfortable. For example, he challenged placing top priority on home and family responsibilities (Luke 9:57-62) and even family itself (Mark 3:31-35). Jesus was called to a life that did not include commitment to a spouse and children. Then and now, disciples of Jesus also have heard and accepted a call not to marry. Though Jesus did not mandate such a life for all his disciples, he did call us all to the sometimes difficult discernment of keeping God our priority amid conflicting demands from family.

Another discomforting priority challenged by Jesus was prejudice. By dining with tax collectors and sinners and journeying to areas where Gentiles lived, Jesus rejected the prejudice seen in the religious leaders and, at times, in the disciples. He was criticized for his association with people the religious leaders labeled "unclean." We may not think of labeling prejudice as a "treasure." However, if we live with prejudice as a priority, it does capture our heart and separate us from God. How can we claim to follow a God of justice, mercy, and love while at the same time blatantly, or subtly, excluding certain people from an equal measure of God's love? Doing so creates an internal conflict that is destructive to our hearts.

Jesus tended his heart by keeping it next to God, his treasure. His own choice was to eschew any wealth whatsoever. He enjoyed the hospitality and generosity of friends and followers, yet as far as we know, he kept no possessions beyond his immediate needs. Though he spoke with authority, he avoided any position of authority or power. Once, after Jesus preached to a large crowd and fed them bread and fish, the people recognized him as a prophet and planned to make him king (John 6:1-15). Jesus, however, went away by himself to a mountain, rejecting this opportunity for power. No attachment separated him from God, including family. In addition to rejecting each of these potential treasures, Jesus did not harbor any prejudice. He extended his compassion and love to women and men, to poor and rich, to powerless and powerful, to young and old, to outcasts and privileged ones.

Jesus did what he needed to do to pursue the ministry to which he had been called. Though he did not insist that all his followers remain unattached to family or refuse any possessions or avoid any position of authority, his own example and his warnings about dangerous attachments serve as guides for us. Jesus' teaching and example call us to be attentive to and in prayer about how we acquire and use our wealth and our power. His words also challenge us to examine the importance of our relationships, our jobs, our prejudices, and other "treasures" that could become a top priority in our lives. Our own discomfort—about a sermon we heard on riches or about the person sitting next to us at a game or concert, for example—may be a signal that we need to examine our "treasures." Jesus said, "No one can serve two masters" (Matthew 6:24). A heart divided between two allegiances will be torn apart. A well-tended heart, however, follows the commandment that Jesus acknowledged was the greatest: Love God with your whole heart.

"He Went to Him"

But wanting to justify himself, he asked Jesus, "And who is my neighbor?" Jesus replied, "A man was going down from Jerusalem to Jericho, and fell into the hands of robbers, who stripped him, beat him, and went away, leaving him half dead. Now by chance a priest was going down that road; and when he saw him, he passed by on the other side. So likewise a Levite, when he came to the place and saw him, passed by on the other side. But a Samaritan while travel-ing came near him; and when he saw him, he was moved with pity. He went to him and bandaged his wounds, having poured oil and wine on them. Then he put him on his own animal, brought him to an inn, and took care of him. The next day he took out two denarii, gave them to the innkeeper, and said, 'Take care of him; and when I come back, I will repay you whatever more you spend.' Which of these three, do you think, was a neighbor to the man who fell into the hands of the robbers?" He said, "The one who showed him mercy." Jesus said to him, "Go and do likewise." (Luke 10:29-37)

A lawyer came to Jesus, asking him about the requirements for eter-nal life. Jesus asked him what the law said. The lawyer responded with the commandments to love God and to love one's neighbor. After Jesus affirms this answer, the lawyer asks the question to which this parable is the answer: "Who is my neighbor?"

How would we answer that question? Our answer would likely be based on location. Our neighbors are the folks living near us. Or, know-ing that God wants us to care about everyone, we might expand our boundaries to include our larger community and even other places around the globe. Jesus, however, changed the focus of "neighbor" when, after telling the parable, he asked the lawyer, "Who was a neigh-bor to the man?" (v. 36). The neighbor was the one who helped. A neighbor, then, is a person who demonstrates compassion. The person living across the street may or may not be my neighbor, just as I may or may not be a neighbor to the people living next door.

This parable has other lessons in its details. Two characters in the story illustrate how priorities may hinder us from being a neighbor. A third character, the Samaritan, is a model for letting God be the priority and for acting in ways that reflect that priority.

We do not know anything about the man on the road to Jericho except that he was a victim of robbers who beat him and left him seriously injured. The man could have been a Jew in good standing in the religious community, or he could have been a Gentile. He was left with no identification and might have been beaten too badly to be recognized or to respond to questions. Three different travelers passed along the same road, and each one saw the man. The text is specific: a priest saw him; a Levite saw him; and a Samaritan saw him. Why did the first two move over and pass on by? Why did the third man stop?

The priest and the Levite were both religious men, leaders in the Jewish community. We can speculate why they did not help. Perhaps they had priorities other than doing what they knew God asked of them, which was to show mercy. Their priorities could have been their positions in the synagogue or temple, or their schedules. If the priest were on his way to teach in the synagogue, he might have thought that his schedule did not permit the delay of stopping to help. After all, who knows how long getting involved in a situation like that might take! Perhaps even more important to both men was the risk of doing something that would make them unclean. They might not be allowed to enter the synagogue at all if they touched this man who may have been covered with blood and may have been an unclean Jew or even a Samaritan. Perhaps they debated briefly in their minds which "law" was more important. They knew that God wanted them to be clean and on time for services. Yes, God had said something about compassion, too, but they may have reasoned that surely God would send along someone else to help that man. After all, they had more important duties to fulfill. We may identify with their dilemma. Even if our intent is to make God and God's will our priority, sometimes our own ideas about what is right can cloud our discernment; and sometimes the right choice simply may not be as obvious to us as we might like it to be.

Look at the Samaritan and consider all the important priorities that he placed below the priority of showing mercy and kindness. First, the

Samaritan stopped and went to the man. Whatever schedule he had to keep, he let go of it at that moment. Being on time for appointments is usually a good thing, but the Samaritan demonstrated his awareness that this other man's life was certainly more important than his schedule.

Second, by stopping, the Samaritan risked his personal safety. As he looked at the injured man, he was staring at the evidence that this was a dangerous road. Perhaps the robbers were still around, waiting for their next victim. One's own safety and security are good priorities, yet should they always be top priority?

The priest and Levite were bound by prejudices and by rules regarding being clean or unclean. Whether or not this was a third priority sacrificed by the Samaritan, we do not know. We do know, however, that he touched and treated the wounded man, who might have been of a different race and religion. The Samaritan also might have risked the transfer of some infection from the bloody wounds. Certainly treating the beaten man and loading him onto his animal might have made a mess of the Samaritan's clothes and possessions.

A fourth priority abandoned by the Samaritan was his own convenience and comfort—including his financial comfort. He took the injured man to an inn and cared for him through the night. He even willingly gave a blank check to the innkeeper. We have no reason to think that the Samaritan was a rich man, yet he generously gave two denarii to the innkeeper and promised to pay whatever the cost of the man's care beyond that initial payment. The Samaritan was not attached to anything more than his desire to show compassion to the man in desperate need. He certainly had his heart in the right place.

We may not think of our jobs, schedules, personal security, rules (religious or otherwise), convenience, or comfort as priorities in our lives. Nevertheless, if we look at our actions, we may find that our attachments to some of these prevent us from being a neighbor. Priorities that interfere with our relationship with God do not tend our hearts well. Perhaps the heart of the priest was troubled as he taught about God and thought about the injured man. Perhaps the Levite had bad dreams that troubled his heart. Of course, we cannot know if misplaced priorities created such problems. Certainly, the Samaritan was clear about his priorities. After concluding the story, Jesus simply said to the lawyer, who had correctly identified the neighbor, "Go and do likewise."

Relationships

Jesus had a wide circle of friends and acquaintances. Some of these people were followers. They had heard him preach on the outskirts of town, or they had heard him teach in the synagogue. A few had been healed by Jesus or were friends or family members of someone else who had been healed. These people wanted to be near Jesus, to hear more of his preaching and teaching, and to help him in his ministry. In general, people wanted to be a friend to Jesus and to claim him as friend.

Others in the wide circle were opponents of Jesus. Some Pharisees sought out Jesus, engaging him in debate in the synagogue or inviting him to dinner. At least in the early days of Jesus' ministry, these opponents must have found Jesus interesting and good company. An evening spent with him in debate no doubt was engaging, challenging, and enjoyable.

Jesus himself expanded the wide circle by befriending "sinners": tax collectors, poor people, and other ignored or excluded members of the society. Jesus did not merely talk about being kind to outcasts in the community. As always, he followed his teaching and preaching with personal action. He even called one outcast—the tax collector, Matthew—to be a trusted member of his inner circle (Matthew 9:9). We read that Jesus accepted Matthew's invitation to dinner and sat to eat with other "tax collectors and sinners" (Matthew 9:10). This meal was likely one of many such occasions. Jesus himself reported what others were saying about him. Not only was he called a "glutton and a drunkard," but also he was accused of being "a friend of tax collectors and sinners" (Matthew 11:19). No doubt, the accusations of the religious leaders about Jesus' company did not trouble him because he wanted to be a friend to these excluded ones.

Given this wide circle of friends and acquaintances, we may assume that Jesus was very sociable, and that he was delightful company. In addition to going to banquets and dinners, Jesus may have stayed in the homes of some of his many followers. This large circle of people around Jesus was a mixed blessing. The sheer number of people wanting Jesus' time and attention surely drained him physically and emotionally. Yet, the dinners with good food, lively conversation, thoughtful discussions, and comfortable surroundings would have tended Jesus' heart well.

One encounter with Jesus' own family raises questions about the nature of their relationship with him. His mother, brothers, and sisters were part of a crowd outside the house where Jesus was staying. They had gone to him in response to the concerns that Jesus had "gone out of his mind" (Mark 3:21). When told that his family was outside calling to him, Jesus questioned, "Who are my mother and my brothers?" (Mark 3:33). He then redefined his family as those who are believers and followers, saying, "Whoever does the will of God is my brother and sister and mother" (Mark 3:35).

In Matthew's account of the same encounter, Jesus' mother and brothers were said to be "standing outside, wanting to speak to him" (12:46). Jesus pointed to his disciples and named them as his mother and brothers (12:49). Why did Jesus not go to speak to his family? Do his words suggest that his mother and brothers were not accepting of God's will for Jesus and themselves? We cannot know, but certainly the gospel accounts suggest reluctance on Jesus' part to speak with his family, and a possible strain in their relationship.

We do not know much else about Jesus' family during the time of his ministry. Only the writer of the Gospel of John placed Jesus' mother, Mary, at the cross. We do know that when Jesus called disciples and other followers, he often asked them to leave all, including family. Apparently he had done so as well. Perhaps his relationships with his own family troubled his heart at times. Yet, if certain family members had opposed what he felt called to be and do, then Jesus' decision to walk away had tended his heart's deepest knowing and had put his heart with his treasure.

Within the wide circle of friends and acquaintances, Jesus had a closer circle of followers whom he chose as friends. First, he chose a "family" of brothers, his disciples, to be with him and work with him in his ministry. He shared both himself and his mission with these twelve. From among these, Jesus chose an even closer inner circle of intimate friends: Peter, James, and John. Other than the disciples, Jesus was close to Mary, Martha, and Lazarus. We do not encounter these two sisters and their brother often in Scripture, but we know from several accounts—the visit recorded briefly in Luke 10:38-42, the extended account surrounding the death of Lazarus in John 11:1-44, and the celebration dinner described in John 12:1-11—that Jesus included these three among his dearest friends. Perhaps he was close to other friends as well. For example, a group of women who followed Jesus and "provided for" him and his disciples are mentioned in Luke 8:1-3. How did Jesus tend his heart in these close relationships with his disciples and other friends?

Jesus tended the needs of his heart by spending private time with his chosen family. He knew that relationships, if they are to survive and thrive, must be nurtured with time together—time spent talking and listening as well as time simply being together. Jesus frequently spent time with only the twelve disciples. For example, they often were alone on a boat crossing the Sea of Galilee (Luke 8:22). Sometimes Jesus took his disciples with him apart from the crowd to pray (Luke 9:18). At other times, Jesus took them up a mountain to teach them—although sometimes the crowd followed (John 6:3-5). In the account of the betrayal in the Gospel of John, we read, "Jesus . . . went out with his disciples across the Kidron valley to a place where there was a garden, which he and his disciples entered. Now Judas . . . also knew the place, because Jesus often met there with his disciples" (John 18:1-2). Jesus and his disciples "often met there." In a garden, on a mountain, and elsewhere, Jesus and his disciples talked, listened, rested, and tended their hearts. Jesus also spent time alone with his closest inner circle: Peter, James, and John. Two memorable occasions were the transfiguration (Matthew 17:1-13) and the final hours of prayer in the garden of Gethsemane before Jesus' arrest (Matthew 26:36-46).

During his time alone with his disciples, Jesus tended his heart by opening it to them. He talked with them about what he was thinking and feeling, including the agony of his own heart. He told them when he was deeply troubled, explaining that he must undergo suffering and that he would be handed over to the chief priests and scribes, condemned to death, and crucified (Matthew 16:21; 20:18-19). Knowing and being known, deeply and intimately, tended all of their emotions, increased understanding, guided decisions, and kept their hearts centered on God. The tending was a two-way street. Certainly Jesus cared for the hearts, minds, bodies, and souls of his closest friends and followers. Surely the twelve leaned on one another for support. And, without a doubt, the disciples helped to tend Jesus' heart.

An American spiritual depicts Jesus' journey as follows:

> Jesus walked this lonesome valley.
> He had to walk it by himself.
> Oh, nobody else could walk it for him.
> He had to walk it by himself.

That is not entirely true. Jesus did not choose to walk that lonesome valley by himself. Yes, he did die on the cross. No one could do *that* for him. Yet throughout his ministry, from the beginning until the end, Jesus invited others to walk the valley, not for him, but with him. Jesus tended his own heart by loving his disciples and other intimate friends, and by being loved in return. At the end of his life, Jesus watched as his disciples abandoned him; but, after his death and resurrection, Jesus tended his heart by forgiving them.

In the Gospel of John, Jesus' forgiveness of Peter is implied by the conversation they have. Three times Jesus asked Peter: "Simon son of John, do you love me?" (21:15, 16, 17). Unlike the three denials by Peter after Jesus' arrest, this time Peter affirmed his love, repeating, "Yes, Lord: you know that I love you" (21:15). Three times Jesus called Peter to the task he needed him to do: "Tend my sheep" (21:16). Then he repeated his first call to Peter, saying, "Follow me" (21:19). Knowing how important reconciliation—the restoration of their friendship—would be to Peter, Jesus forgave him. This gift of reconciliation would have tended Jesus' heart, too. Also, Jesus needed for Peter to reclaim the call to follow and to become the rock on which Jesus' church would be built (Matthew 16:18).

Jesus expressed his need of all his disciples when he said to them, "Go therefore and make disciples of all nations" (Matthew 28:19). He entrusted to them the ministry he had begun. From the first call to the last, Jesus nurtured his relationships with these dear friends. After his death and resurrection, he wanted to see them because he needed them and he loved them still.

"The Lord Turned and Looked at Peter"

Then they seized him and led him away, bringing him into the high priest's house. But Peter was following at a distance. When they had kindled a fire in the middle of the courtyard and sat down together, Peter sat among them. Then a servant-girl, seeing him in the firelight, stared at him and said, "This man also was with him." But he denied it, saying, "Woman, I do not know him." A little later someone else, on seeing him, said, "You also are one of them." But Peter said, "Man, I am not!" Then about an hour later still another kept insisting, "Surely this man also was with him; for he is a Galilean." But Peter said, "Man, I do not know what you are talking about!" At that moment, while he was still speaking, the cock crowed. The Lord turned and looked at Peter. Then Peter remembered the word of the Lord, how he had said to him, "Before the cock crows today, you will deny me three times." And he went out and wept bitterly. (Luke 22:54-62)

As he began his ministry, Jesus called Peter and his brother Andrew away from their jobs as fishermen. Jesus chose Peter to be a disciple, and Peter chose to follow. He became a main character in the Gospels—the disciple from whom we hear the most and about whom we observe the most. In fact, Peter, along with James and John, was in Jesus' innermost circle. These three disciples were with Jesus for experiences from which the other disciples were excluded. You might say that Peter was like a brother, close friend, and trusted coworker all rolled into one. Perhaps by looking carefully at Peter and his interaction with Jesus, we can better understand how this relationship tended the hearts of each.

Peter was impulsive and eager. He almost always led with his heart, speaking and acting out of emotion rather than careful thought. When Jesus walked out on the water to meet the disciples in the boat, for example, Peter wanted to walk on water, too (Matthew 14:22-23). Peter, however, wanted Jesus to call him out onto the water. He sounded almost like a young child, asking his daddy to call him off the edge of the swimming pool to paddle to his father's outstretched arms. Perhaps Peter thought that if Jesus told him to jump in, that would mean the venture would be safe. Jesus said, "Come," and Peter started walking to Jesus; but he began to sink once he became frightened. When he started crying out for Jesus to save him, Jesus grabbed Peter's hand and pulled him up. Might Jesus have been smiling through all of this? Peter's impulsiveness and intensity were, no doubt, a challenge at times, yet Jesus must have enjoyed the youthful exuberance and sheer delight of Peter.

On the Mount of Transfiguration, Peter was once again impulsive as he offered to build three houses—one each for Jesus, Moses, and Elijah (Matthew 17:1-8). Again Peter wanted Jesus to give permission, saying to Jesus, "If you wish" (Matthew 17:4). Perhaps Jesus again was smiling at Peter, at his impulsive energy and his understatement that "it is good for us to be here" (Matthew 17:4). Surely Peter's enthusiasm warmed and delighted Jesus' heart. As on the water, however, Peter, along with James and John, became frightened. A cloud appeared and a voice spoke. Once again Jesus' touch provided comfort and security. His calming and comforting hand, along with his voice of wisdom and reason, were good for Peter's heart.

Peter was a leader—perhaps *the* leader—among the disciples. Whenever a smaller group of disciples was drawn apart by Jesus, Peter was always included. In addition to the time on the Mount of Transfiguration, several other experiences were shared only by Peter, James, and John. These three disciples witnessed the raising of Jairus's daughter from the dead (Mark 5:35-43), and they stayed closer to Jesus while he prayed in the garden of Gethsemane (Matthew 26:36-46). Peter's leadership also was evidenced by the many questions he asked Jesus. Perhaps he was the spokesperson for the others who were reluctant to confront Jesus (e.g., Matthew 15:15; 18:21). Peter also was the first to announce this confession to Jesus: "You are the Messiah, the Son of the living God" (Matthew 16:16). Whether he was a spokesman presenting a conclusion reached by all the disciples or he was speaking for himself with unusual thought and reflection, we do not know. What we do know is that Jesus returned the affirmation and encouragement by blessing Peter and announcing, "You are Peter, and on this rock I will build my church" (Matthew 16:18).

Immediately following this text, although perhaps somewhat later in time, we see that Peter was not always the supporter that Jesus needed. When Jesus spoke of his suffering to come, Peter said, "This must never happen to you" (Matthew 16:22). Jesus did not hesitate to rebuke Peter for getting in his way, for making the path ahead more difficult. Surely, however, Jesus must have understood that a heartfelt expression of concern and protection was behind Peter's words. In spite of Peter's occasional lapses in good judgment, he remained a leader among the disciples. Jesus must have recognized and valued Peter's strengths and appreciated his ability to lead.

One of Peter's least attractive characteristics was his bravado, which he displayed most clearly during the intimate and emotional evening of Jesus' arrest. Following the Passover meal and before going to Gethsemane, Peter seemed to place himself and his loyalty above that of the other disciples when he announced, "Though all become deserters because of you, I will never desert you" (Matthew 26:33). Jesus warned that Peter would deny him, but Peter plowed ahead with confidence, saying, "Even though I must die with you, I will not deny you" (Matthew 26:35). As it turned out, the evening was not a good one for Peter. First, he, along with James and John, failed Jesus by falling asleep in the garden after he had been asked to pray with and for Jesus. Later, after Jesus' arrest, Peter did, in fact, deny knowing Jesus, not once but three times.

The cock crowed. Jesus "turned and looked at Peter. Then Peter remembered" (Luke 22:61). The scene described in these verses is heartbreaking. The poignant moment surely broke two hearts. The best friend and Messiah whom Peter had followed for three years had been arrested like a common criminal. The close friend and right-hand man whom Jesus had relied on had denied knowing the one he had followed. Peter had failed Jesus again, this time in a more significant way than in the garden.

The scene tells us as much about tending hearts as it does about breaking hearts. Imagine it with me. Jesus looked at Peter; Peter looked back. Both peered into the eyes of the other. Both remembered. Perhaps the moment was so painful because of the ways each had tended the heart of the other through the years—carefully, constantly, deeply. They knew each other so well and had so much to remember. They loved each other so much. No wonder the denial hurt.

Peter wept bitterly, feeling overwhelming regret for having denied knowing the one he had followed and loved. Jesus must have been hurt by the denial, too, but surely he hurt for Peter as well. After all, he knew Peter well enough to have predicted that Peter's strength would fail him when he felt threatened. Soon, however, Jesus' attention was turned to a different kind of pain—the physical pain of flogging. Nevertheless, the fact that they knew each other intimately, remembered the years of their relationship, and still loved each other may have tended their hearts even as they experienced the pain of that moment.

As we feel the emotion of this moment between Jesus and Peter, our own experiences of loss and pain may come to our minds and hearts. Sometimes healing from a loss begins when we recognize that the depth of our pain is related to the depth of love we experienced in the relationship that tended our heart so well.

How did Jesus tend his heart in his relationship with Peter? He opened himself to be known by him and to know him. He loved Peter for who he was—from strong leader to impulsive child and every aspect in between. Jesus called out and affirmed the best in Peter. Although he did not ignore Peter's faults and failings, Jesus always forgave him. Jesus' friendship with Peter is a model of acceptance and forgiveness to be practiced in every relationship. Jesus not only loved Peter but also received Peter's love in return. Giving and receiving acceptance and love are equally important for our own relationships.

For three years, Jesus and Peter ministered alongside one another—risking, trusting, and loving. The painful looking and remembering after the cock crowed for the third time was not the final scene. According to a postresurrection account in the Gospel of John, Peter once again displayed his eagerness by jumping off a boat into the sea to swim quickly to shore to meet Jesus (John 21:7). Perhaps Jesus smiled once again to see Peter's enthusiasm. These two friends, Jesus and Peter, were a good team. They tended each other's heart very well.

Questions for Reflection and Discussion

1. We considered how Jesus tended his heart in the way he dealt with four emotions he experienced: anger, grief, passion, and compassion. List some of the ways we may respond to these emotions. What helpful examples did you see in the ways that Jesus dealt with these emotions? What first step might you take to better deal with your own emotion(s) in light of Jesus' example(s)?

2. Why is it important for us to tend our emotions? What can happen when an emotion goes untended?

3. Are you holding an untended emotion in your own heart? Symptoms of an untended emotion might include one or more of the following: unusual physical distress, sleepless nights, strained relationships, distraction during prayer or neglected prayer time, and questions from friends and family (e.g, "Is everything OK?" or "You don't seem like yourself"). If you are holding an untended emotion, why do you think you are unable or unwilling to let go? What damage to yourself or to others do you think has resulted from this untended emotion? What steps might you take to deal with this emotion in ways that will tend your heart?

4. Can you think of another emotion, other than those discussed here, that you recognize in Jesus? How did he tend this emotion?

5. Jesus showed compassion to the vulnerable and excluded persons in his society. Who in our culture are the excluded or neglected ones needing our compassion? Following Jesus' example of compassion that requires action, how, specifically, might you extend compassion to those you have identified?

6. Return to the parable of the Prodigal Son. In what ways did the characters in this story tend their hearts? In your own life, is there a "younger son" who has made bad choices or an "older son" who is jealous and resentful—whether a relative or not—to whom you need to extend compassion? What can you do to show compassion to this individual? If the person accepts your compassion, what healing might occur? If the person refuses your compassion, how will you feel? How will you respond?

7. Passion can be defined as what one is committed to or enthusiastic about. According to this definition, how would you describe Jesus' passion? How did he express this passion? Identify one thing about which you personally are passionate. If you cannot think of anything, ask someone to suggest a passion he or she may see in you. How are you expressing this passion? If you are not expressing this passion, what hinders you?

8. Why are our checkbooks and our calendars good indicators of our priorities? Look at your own checkbook and the calendar on which you record your schedule of commitments. What do these reveal about your priorities? Could you comfortably

label these priorities as your "treasures"? Why or why not? In what ways do you experience your heart "residing" with these treasures?

9. According to the parable of the Good Samaritan, what was Jesus' definition of a neighbor? What person or persons need you to be their neighbor? What keeps you from being a neighbor?

10. How do relationships tend our hearts? What are some ways we can nurture our relationships? What relationships tend your own heart best? Do you spend enough time with these persons to nurture the relationships? Identify the specific characteristics of these relationships that tend your heart. How can you cultivate these characteristics?

3. Tending the Mind

THE APOSTLE PAUL WROTE TO THE CHURCH AT PHILIPPI: "LET THE SAME mind be in you that was in Christ Jesus" (Philippians 2:5). What does having the mind of Jesus mean for us? Paul's explanation likens Jesus to a slave, humble and obedient to the will of God, which ultimately meant death on a cross. Paul suggests that having the mind of Jesus reflects an attitude, an intention. What can we observe about the mind of Jesus from the Gospels? We may not think of Jesus as an intellectual, but the reaction of the crowd, including the scholars of his day, to his teaching suggests he was brilliant. We may think of Jesus as a "solid rock," but some people said that he was out of his mind (Mark 3:21; John 10:20). How would we describe Jesus' mind, and what do we know about how he tended it?

Jesus did have an extraordinary mind. On many occasions, including when he was a mere twelve-year-old child in the temple, he amazed and astounded other teachers. Further evidence of his exceptional intellect is illustrated in numerous encounters when he totally confounded the religious leaders. Another indication of his well-above-average intelligence may be found in the number of times his disciples failed to understand what he was trying to teach them. At times he appeared impatient or even angry with their inability to grasp his meaning, suggesting the possibility that these men may not have been very smart. In any case, it's evident that Jesus' intellect was far superior.

Perhaps we do not often refer to Jesus as an intellectual because his mental abilities, his giftedness, went far beyond scholarship. For one thing, Jesus was unusually perceptive. His intuition and insight into the feelings and thoughts of others were extraordinary. More than once we are told that Jesus knew what others were thinking (e.g., Matthew 12:25). Jesus also was very wise. As the brief sentence about his childhood reminds us, "Jesus increased in wisdom" (Luke 2:52). Jesus' wisdom, though sometimes unconventional, was manifest in his good judgment. We might say that he had good common sense, as when he allowed his hungry disciples to pluck and eat grain from the fields despite laws prohibiting such activity on the Sabbath (Matthew 12:1). Furthermore, we recognize Jesus' wisdom in his reinterpretation of the law. In the Sermon on the Mount, for example, Jesus frequently used the two-part phrase, "You have heard it said . . . but I say . . ." (Matthew 5).

How did Jesus tend his mind—take care of, sharpen, and nurture it—so that he could apply it to its fullest? He knew that the mind, like the body, needs both exercise and rest. In the gospel accounts we see that Jesus demonstrated many ways to exercise the mind, including debating and storytelling. Likewise, he demonstrated various ways to aid mental rest, such as getting adequate physical rest, avoiding unnecessary complexity in one's lifestyle, and lessening worry and anxiety—even when surrounded by stressful circumstances. In fact, Jesus was explicit in telling his disciples not to worry even when in danger but, instead, to trust the Holy Spirit to teach them how to respond to accusers (Luke 12:11). By his own example, he taught them how wit or humor not only exercises the mind but also provides release and relaxation from tension in mind and body.

Another aspect of tending the mind that Jesus illustrated is pausing to reflect—as he did when the Pharisees brought before him a woman accused of adultery (John 8:1-11). By counting the cost before speaking or acting, we can avoid many mistakes and regrets and, therefore, better tend not only our minds but also our bodies, hearts, and souls. Similarly, Jesus recognized the need to keep our minds open and be willing to change our minds, if necessary, once we have a clear vision of God's will. For example, he often rebuked the Pharisees for refusing to listen, to reconsider prior assumptions, and to change their minds.

Consider again the commandment that Jesus said was the greatest: "You shall love the Lord your God with all your heart, and with all your soul, and with all your mind, and with all your strength" (Mark 12:30). While we probably recognize the necessity of using our mind to love God, we may not have thought about the need for intentional tending of our mind. Looking at the ways Jesus tended his mind can teach us how to have healthier minds that are better equipped to know and understand God's call to us, including the call to love God.

Exercise

In the same way that the body needs exercise so that it may work to its full potential, the mind needs consistent and vigorous exercise. Minds must be active, engaged, creative, and challenged in order to be healthy. That may not happen without intentional exercise. Did Jesus tend his mind as intentionally as he tended his body and heart? Yes, he did. Although the time Jesus spent developing his mind may not be recorded explicitly, the evidence that Jesus had a very keen mind—kept sharp through regular exercise—is found throughout the Gospels.

One way to exercise the mind is to read. Certainly Jesus read or listened attentively as others read. Luke's account of Jesus as a twelve-year-old boy indicates that he had a remarkable knowledge and under-standing of Scripture at a very young age. Years later, in preparation for beginning his ministry, Jesus spent forty days in the wilderness where he was tempted by Satan. According to the gospel accounts, Jesus used Scripture in his arguments against Satan, revealing an ability to recall and recite Scripture and apply it appropriately in defense of an argument. Such skill clearly indicates regular exercise of the mind.

During his ministry, Jesus continued to give evidence of his thorough knowledge of and insight into Scripture. In Matthew, for example, we read that Jesus challenged the Pharisees, saying, "Have you not read what David did . . . ?" (Matthew 12:3). Again Jesus asked the Pharisees, "Have you not read in the law . . . ?" (Matthew 12:5). Often Jesus cited Scripture as he confronted the Jewish teachers and other leaders, who supposedly were the expert authorities in such matters. Furthermore, he interpreted the Scripture in new and surprising ways.

Jesus' active mind also was evidenced by the powerful, engaging, cre-ative, and vivid stories he told—his parables. Jesus was an attentive observer of everything around him. Always he listened, heard, and observed. With keen senses and sensitivity, Jesus processed carefully the data his mind had collected. He developed memorable stories and vivid metaphors based on familiar, daily life to provide lessons about

God and about how God calls people to live. Whether describing a Samaritan on the road to Jericho, a vineyard owner paying wages to day laborers, or a young man squandering his inheritance, Jesus was a masterful storyteller.

Without question, Jesus had the active mind of a gifted teacher. He did not merely present his brilliant stories and then, as some professors do, gather his notes and leave the "classroom." No, Jesus asked questions of his hearers, challenging them to engage their minds and inviting them to ask further questions. After telling the story of the Good Samaritan, for example, Jesus asked, "Which of these three, do you think, was a neighbor . . . ? (Luke 10:36). Likewise, when the disciples came to Jesus asking for an explanation of the parable of the Sower, he gave an explanation and then described further the kingdom of heaven. Then he asked them, "Have you understood all this?" (Matthew 13:51). Notice when reading the Gospels how many times Jesus asked his listeners, "What do you think?"

Yet more evidence that Jesus exercised his mind is seen in the way he debated his enemies. One of his techniques was to fire back a question in response to a question asked primarily to trap him. In response to a question of his authority, Jesus said, "I will also ask you a question, and you tell me: Did the baptism of John come from heaven, or was it of human origin?" (Luke 20:3). Or, when the Pharisees asked why the disciples did not follow the ritual washing before eating, Jesus questioned them: "And why do you break the commandment of God for the sake of your tradition?" (Matthew 15:3). Jesus was attentive, thoughtful, mentally quick, and perceptive. He put himself in positions where scholars would engage and challenge him.

How did Jesus tend his mind? He followed a vigorous exercise routine of reading, observing, storytelling, teaching, and debating. Jesus' mind was a match for anyone he encountered. To tend our own minds, we must follow his example in many ways. Here is one essential directive for each of us: *Exercise your mind.*

"Do Not Do as They Do"

Then Jesus said to the crowds and to his disciples, "The scribes and the Pharisees sit on Moses' seat; therefore, do whatever they teach you and follow it; but do not do as they do, for they do not practice what they teach. They tie up heavy burdens, hard to bear, and lay them on the shoulders of others; but they themselves are unwilling to lift a finger to move them. They do all their deeds to be seen by others; for they make their phylacteries broad and their fringes long. They love to have the place of honor at banquets and the best seats in the synagogues, and to be greeted with respect in the market-places, and to have people call them rabbi." (Matthew 23:1-7)

One's greatest virtue is sometimes one's vice as well. Discipline in regular exercise and healthy eating is exemplary, yet some people carry vigorous exercise and dietary restrictions to such an extreme that they endanger their health. Showing compassion for those who are hungry or sick is certainly a virtue, but "selfless" service to others without time out for renewal can lead to physical and emotional burnout. Tending the whole self requires a healthy balance. Exercise must be balanced by rest. Showing compassion for others needs the balance of relationships and times of solitude. Such offsetting activities can provide balance for the body, heart, mind, or soul. A person, however, is not the sum of isolated parts. Tending for the whole person requires balance not only within but also among *all* the parts. Body, heart, mind, and soul must be in harmony with one another.

In this passage we read of men who have sharp minds tended by regular exercise. Their words and practices, however, suggest that their hearts and souls are not providing balance for their minds. The scribes and the Pharisees were very knowledgeable about the law and all Scripture. They read and studied and taught. Yet Jesus bestowed no praise on them—or on other religious leaders. Time after time we read of the Pharisees and Sadducees challenging Jesus, using their knowledge of Scripture and other Jewish law to test him and try to trap him. Where did these Scripture-quoting religious men go wrong? Perhaps in examining Jesus' criticism of these teachers and scholars, we can be alerted to potential dangers from getting out of balance.

Jesus' first charge in this passage from Matthew 23 is clear. The scribes and Pharisees "do not practice what they teach" (v. 3). In the verses that follow, Jesus offers a scathing attack on these learned men. He begins the charges with, "Woe to you, scribes and Pharisees, hypocrites!" (v. 13). With angry words, Jesus enumerates his accusations. For example, the scribes and Pharisees "tithe mint, dill, and cummin, and have neglected the weightier matters of the law: justice and mercy and faith" (v. 23). They have carefully followed rules regarding ritual cleansing on the outside, but they are "full of greed and self-indulgence" on the inside (v. 25). They follow the letter of the law; their failure comes from their obsession with the letter rather than the spirit of the law. At one point Jesus describes their problem as being "their hardness of heart" (Mark 3:5). Their hearts are not open to balancing their concern for the law with compassion for others.

A second charge Jesus makes is that the religious leaders unnecessarily burden others. They use their narrow, rigid interpretation of the law to exclude others from full participation in the Jewish community. Not even Jesus and his disciples can escape the accusation that they are breaking Jewish law and, therefore, are not pure and acceptable Jews before God. They accuse Jesus and the disciples of associating with obviously "unclean" Gentiles and sinners, not following the laws regarding fasting and washing, and not observing the Sabbath restrictions. If Jesus and his disciples are condemned for their negligence, we can only imagine the rejection that must be experienced by the poor, the sick, and others unable to know—much less follow fully—all the intricacies of the law. The religious leaders rigidly impose on others the details of the law without balance from the soul's offering of God's grace.

The third indictment Jesus levels at the scribes and Pharisees is that they lack humility. Elsewhere Jesus enumerates religious practices—giving alms, praying, and fasting—that are done by some to impress others rather than to honor God (Matthew 6:1-16). As Jesus says here, the Pharisees want the best seats in the house, whether at a dinner party or in the synagogue. They want attention. They want the praise, privilege, and respect they think they have earned. Again, they lack balance. They use their minds to know the law, yet the mind alone cannot know God.

Unlike the Pharisees, Jesus is a model for practicing what he preaches, lifting the burdens of others, and exemplifying humility. Jesus feeds the hungry and heals the sick. He forgives others. He is not anxious about his life. He prays in private. He loves God, and he loves his neighbor as himself. In all these ways, Jesus demonstrates what he preaches and teaches. He tries to remove the burdens others carry and the barriers they face in trying to be part of the religious community. In healing those with mental illnesses, leprosy, blindness, and other physical problems, he accomplishes both the easing of burdens and the removal of barriers. He invites *all* who are burdened to come to him, saying, "Take my yoke upon you, and learn from me; for I am gentle and humble in heart, and you will find rest for your souls" (Matthew 11:29). Always, Jesus is humble. He does not use his brilliant mind, his gifts, or his power to exploit others or to gain privilege.

Both the Pharisees and Jesus exercise their minds. The difference between them has less to do with their minds and more to do with their hearts and souls. Jesus says that the pure in heart will see God (Matthew 5:8). The Pharisees say purity is a matter of the law. They refuse to see God in—or extend God's grace to—anyone who does not meet their standard.

Again and again Jesus warns the crowd and his disciples about the religious leaders who do not practice what they preach, who burden others, and who lack humility. We may see these failings in others and even in ourselves. May we hear again Jesus' words of caution: "Do not do as they do" (Matthew 23:3). We must tend our minds with vigorous exercise, yet we must not let our minds dominate all our words and actions. To be whole, healthy children of God, we must seek to balance body, heart, mind, and soul. As Paul encourages us, "Let the same mind be in you that was in Christ Jesus" (Philippians 2:5).

Rest

As is true for the body, the mind needs rest as well as exercise. Nonstop activity does not tend the mind well. Even the most creative and brilliant minds can become distracted, slower, and prone to error if never allowed to rest. Resting the body, however, does not always rest the mind. We can try to relax in a comfortable, reclining chair and yet never truly rest if our minds are racing through endless "to do" lists or cycling around a worry or two. Our anxious minds can actually prevent us from releasing the tension gripping our bodies, leaving us exhausted and unable to focus on what really matters. There's no doubt that worry, anxiety, and obsessions create stress that harms body, heart, and soul. A troubled mind can make a peaceful soul elusive and a joyful heart unavailable. Jesus was well aware of the danger of worry and the need to rest the mind. He not only tended his own mind with rest but also revealed by example and instruction how we can do the same.

Jesus, who understood the human condition, had clear and direct words to say about worry: "Do not worry about your life, what you will eat or what you will drink, or about your body, what you will wear. . . . Do not worry about tomorrow, for tomorrow will bring worries of its own" (Matthew 6:25, 34). In between these two verses, he addressed the futility of worrying, implying that certainly we should not worry about anything—even our most basic needs. Before looking carefully at Jesus' message about worry, we may react defensively. *Don't worry? That's easy for Jesus to say! What does he know about worry? He never had to face what we face. The stock market falls and threatens the security of our retirement. A company buyout results in our job being phased out. We face tense days waiting to get the results of our exploratory medical tests. Our teenage son will not get into college with the grades he is making. Our teenage daughter has a boyfriend who is sure to be trouble. Our marriage is falling apart. Those are things to worry about! How can we possibly rest our minds?*

Again we ask, *What did Jesus know about worry?* Well, Jesus had crowds following him everywhere, all the time, even when he needed to be alone. At times the crowds were so large that they could have crushed him (Mark 3:9). These overwhelming crowds of people who needed his teaching and healing threatened to exhaust him physically and emotionally. The people in his own hometown took offense at him and rejected him. The Pharisees plotted to entrap him and tried to do so on numerous occasions. The religious leaders conspired to arrest and kill him. He faced constant stress from the growing number of enemies who wanted to get rid of him—permanently. Jesus had plenty to worry about! Yet, the gospel accounts do not describe an anxious or worried Jesus. So, how did Jesus respond when reasons for worry invaded his mind?

One way that Jesus minimized potential worries, thereby resting his mind, was in pursuing a simple lifestyle. He did not own land or a house or an extensive wardrobe. On the contrary, he lived simply and traveled lightly and told his disciples to do the same. We do not need to live exactly as Jesus did, however, in order to follow his example of simplicity. Do we worry about the house payment because we have bought a bigger house than we can afford? If so, we need to downsize. Are we worried about meeting the project deadline at work, being on time to pick up the children, making it to the board meeting, planning/buying/cooking supper, making those calls for the church committee, being available to help with homework, and so on? We keep going over this list of things we must do by bedtime! Perhaps we need to simplify, to lessen the overload that makes mental rest impossible.

Another way Jesus lessened the potential for destructive worries to capture his mind was by being proactive. In other words, when confronted with things worth genuine concern, he faced these challenges head on and shared his concerns with his closest friends and with God. For example, Jesus could have avoided his enemies—the Pharisees, Sadducees, priests, and others—and worried all the time about what they were thinking and doing; instead, he confronted them, debating and correcting them about the law. He refused to change his ministry in any way to protect himself from them. He also talked with his disciples often about these enemies. Talking to trusted friends can provide perspective, new insight, support, encouragement, and comfort. Perhaps Jesus found talking with his disciples to be helpful in these ways. Certainly he found guidance and strength for dealing with his enemies while praying about and for them.

Another challenge Jesus faced head on—one he revealed to his disciples on several occasions—was his own suffering and death. He did not want his disciples to take action to attempt to prevent the events he described. In fact, when Peter adamantly stated that such terrible events should not be allowed, Jesus rebuked him sharply (Matthew 16:22-23). Jesus did want his disciples, however, to support him in what he faced. In the garden of Gethsemane, when the time of betrayal was near, he asked all his disciples to wait with him while he prayed; and he asked three of them specifically to pray with him. We may speculate that perhaps he did worry some about what he faced based on Matthew's description of Jesus being "grieved and agitated" in the garden (26:37). Nevertheless, he found rest for his mind and strength for his journey through prayer. As he had done with lesser challenges throughout his ministry, Jesus actively confronted this difficult moment, saying to his disciples, "Get up, let us be going. See, my betrayer is at hand" (26:46).

Jesus limited potential worries by simplifying his life. Jesus also lessened the potential for destructive worries to capture his mind by proactively confronting his greatest challenges and sharing his burdens with his disciples and with God. Yet another way to limit destructive worries and help the mind rest is suggested in Jesus' teaching. After admonishing his listeners not to worry about food, Jesus said, "Look at the birds of the air; they neither sow nor reap nor gather into barns, and yet your heavenly Father feeds them" (Matthew 6:26). After asking why they worried about clothing, Jesus advised, "Consider the lilies of the field, how they grow; they neither toil nor spin, yet I tell you, even Solomon in all his glory was not clothed like one of these" (Matthew 6:28-29). Jesus told them not to worry but, instead, to look at the birds and consider the lilies.

How may this lessen our worry and rest our minds? First, focusing on something outside ourselves may distract us from our worry. Second, observing the beauty and wonder of God's creation may call us to appreciate the larger world, remember what really matters, and put our worries in proper perspective. Third, looking and considering can be part of a time of reflection and meditation that calms the mind and eases anxiety.

Jesus tells us not to worry and calls us to consider God's creation. So, consider a symphony or a folk song. Consider stroking a child's soft hair. Consider smelling mountain air. Consider what you see or hear or touch or smell. Appreciate, give thanks for, and delight in the experiences of your senses. Perhaps this time spent considering, this time of being with God, is the secret to not being anxious—and, consequently, part of the secret to resting our minds.

"You Are Worried and Distracted by Many Things"

Now as they went on their way, he entered a certain village, where a woman named Martha welcomed him into her home. She had a sister named Mary, who sat at the Lord's feet and listened to what he was saying. But Martha was distracted by her many tasks; so she came to him and asked, "Lord, do you not care that my sister has left me to do all the work by myself? Tell her then to help me." But the Lord answered her, "Martha, Martha, you are worried and distracted by many things; there is need of only one thing. Mary has chosen the better part, which will not be taken away from her." (Luke 10:38-42)

Martha appears in the Gospels on three separate occasions. On the first occasion, she welcomes Jesus into her home (Luke 10:38-42). The next recorded meeting of Martha and Jesus occurs after her brother, Lazarus, has died and Martha has gone out to meet Jesus on his way to the village (John 11:1-44). The third time they meet is again in Martha's home (John 12:1-8). She is giving a dinner party in Jesus' honor because he has raised Lazarus from the dead. Thus, on two occasions when Martha is described, she is the hostess, welcoming a special guest, or many guests, to a dinner party.

In the passage in Luke's Gospel, Martha appears to be busy in the kitchen preparing the meal. At the next dinner, we learn only that "Martha served" (John 12:2). A too casual reading of the passage in Luke may lead us to conclude that Jesus is not only criticizing Martha, but also choosing Mary—her personality, her actions, her spirit—over Martha. Too often the "sit-at-the-feet" role chosen by Mary is lifted up over the homemaker role attributed to Martha. Before accepting that traditional reading, we need to look more carefully at Martha in the context of all we see of her and hear from her. We need also to look more closely at Jesus and his interactions with Martha.

In the passage from Luke, when Jesus enters "a certain village," later identified as Bethany, Martha is the one who welcomes him. Whether Jesus has met Martha, Mary, or Lazarus before, we do not know. The text suggests that Martha may be the one who initiated this visit. In their more traditional roles, Lazarus might have heard Jesus preach, invited him to come to his home, and told his sister to prepare a meal. However, no mention is made here of Lazarus. The sisters appear to be hosting this visit without their brother. Martha may have heard Jesus preach—or at least heard about him from others in her village—and sent word that he would be welcome in her home. Perhaps the later dinner party given to honor Jesus was Martha's idea as well.

The passage most revealing of Martha's character is the longer one in the Gospel of John describing the events surrounding Jesus' raising of Lazarus from the dead. When Lazarus becomes ill, Martha and Mary send word to Jesus. The message to Jesus, and the gospel writer's words describing Jesus' response, indicate the mutual closeness and affection between Jesus and this family. The sisters send this word: "Lord, he whom you love is ill" (John 11:3). We read that "though Jesus loved Martha and her sister and Lazarus . . . he stayed two days longer in the place where he was" (John 11:5). When Jesus does journey toward Bethany, word of his approach reaches Martha and Mary. They are now in mourning because their brother already has died. Other Jews have gathered with the two grieving sisters. According to the custom of the day, the women are expected to stay in their home while mourners come to grieve with them. Martha, however, slips out and goes by herself to meet Jesus. Mary, we are told, stays at home. This one action suggests that perhaps Martha is the strong and adventurous one of the family. She is flying out of her home, contrary to what is proper and expected, to do something she thinks far more important.

When Martha finds Jesus, she tells him boldly, "Lord, if you had been here, my brother would not have died" (John 11:21). Beyond that, she makes a firm confession of her faith that God will grant whatever Jesus asks. What follows is a brief exchange about resurrection. Mary may be known as the one sitting at Jesus feet, but here Martha is the one who confronts him and discusses theology!

Throughout the passage in John 11, Martha is the one who speaks and who acts. Mary's only words, once Martha has retrieved her from the house, are an echo of what Martha already has said to Jesus. When Jesus says to roll away the stone at the entrance of Lazarus' tomb, Martha's pragmatic side is revealed when she cautions that the smell will be unbearable now that Lazarus has been dead four days. Again, Martha appears to be the one with the strength and presence to deal directly with Jesus.

When we read all three passages with stories about Mary and Martha, we get a better picture of these women than what is often preached using only the text in Luke. Martha seems to be an energetic, productive, strong woman of faith who does not hover silently in the kitchen. She gets out and about, knows what is going on, listens, and thinks about serious issues. In comparison, Mary appears to be quiet, contemplative, and passionate. She sits at Jesus' feet; she weeps; she pours perfume on Jesus' feet and wipes them with her hair. Jesus does not choose Mary over Martha. He does, however, try to help Martha recognize one of her faults.

Jesus says to Martha, "You are worried and distracted by many things" (Luke 10:41). He does not criticize her for being a wonderful hostess and cook. In fact, he goes to her house and returns at least once in part because of these very gifts she offers so generously. Martha's problem seems to be not knowing when to stop, not knowing when enough is enough. Martha has become so obsessed with the details of her "to do" list that she whines to Jesus about Mary not helping. Martha wants to sit down with Jesus, but she cannot let go of what she has convinced herself she must do. Jesus knows that worrying is harmful to body, heart, mind, and soul. He wants to help Martha let go of her worries and distractions and focus on what is more important— time with him. Perhaps Jesus finds Martha's constant busyness some- what stressful himself. No doubt he will enjoy the delicious meal that Martha has prepared, but surely he also looks forward to a relaxing evening and the warm company of these dear friends.

Jesus affirms Martha and her gifts by coming to her home, enjoying her hospitality, and talking with her about subjects typically reserved for discussions among men. Jesus affirms Mary by defending her choice to listen that evening and her choice to anoint his feet at the later dinner party. The gifts of *both* women are needed. Perhaps Jesus' words to Martha are not a sharp rebuke spoken loudly from across the room. Perhaps, instead, he goes to her and speaks with gentle under- standing and concern. His words to her are also to us: "Martha, quit worrying! You have done enough. Let those distractions go. Please, for now, come and be with me."

Wit

The writer of the Gospel of Luke records that Jesus said, "Blessed are you who weep now, for you shall laugh" (6:21b). All three Synoptic Gospels record that the people laughed at Jesus when he said that the young girl was only sleeping, that she was not dead (e.g., Matthew 9:24). Nowhere in the Gospels, however, do we read that Jesus laughed—or even smiled. We should note that no mention is made of Jesus having a solemn countenance or a frown on his face, either. Yet why are we often more reluctant to imagine Jesus laughing? Do we tend to associate spiritual things with serious words, tone, and expression? Perhaps we allow for rejoicing, joy, and gladness because these expressions often have a spiritual context. Naturally we want Jesus to rejoice in the Lord and to have joy in his heart, but do we think Jesus may have laughed out loud at a funny story? Would Jesus ever have told a funny story himself? Would he have used a witty response in an otherwise serious argument?

Did Jesus have a sense of humor? If we read his words with that possibility in mind, particularly his numerous exchanges with the Jewish religious leaders, we may discover a man with not only a quick mind but also a razor-sharp wit. If we allow for an occasional sly smile on his face and an ever-so-slight tone of sarcasm in his voice, we may find that Jesus tended his mind by using his wit—his humor—to diffuse otherwise tense situations. Jesus was constantly confronted and attacked, debated and berated, by the Pharisees. Surely a witty retort would have eased Jesus' own frustration with these religious leaders who displayed little openness to his message. Consider, as well, the men with whom Jesus was working and living. Among his disciples were several fishermen, including one who was impulsive and prone to anger and stubbornness. Surely other disciples—perhaps more fishermen, as well as those of different professions—were hard to handle. These men were not religious scholars devoted to serious study of the law! How did Jesus put up with such a crew? All these men, and Jesus himself, needed some fun—play, jokes, and laughter—to tend their minds. A little laughter would have tended their hearts as well, both literally and figuratively.

The religious leaders frequently tried to trap Jesus, to prove him a fraud, or to force him to contradict or break some law. Jesus, in turn, often used his quick wit to outsmart them. While his words are not funny, nor are they meant to be, Jesus' creativity and cleverness in beating the Pharisees at their own game surely delighted his followers. In the retelling, surely the thrill of victory brought a smile or two to the faces of the disciples—and perhaps Jesus' as well. Consider, for example, the time when the Pharisees approached Jesus to, according to the text, "entrap him" (Matthew 22:15-22). First, the spokesman delivered a series of patronizing compliments to Jesus, saying, "Teacher, we know that you are sincere, and teach the way of God in accordance with truth, and show deference to no one; for you do not regard people with partiality" (v. 16). Surely the disciples rolled their eyes at that! Next, the hard question was posed: "Is it lawful to pay taxes to the emperor, or not?" (v. 17). Then, with a clever bit of show and tell, Jesus held up a coin with the emperor's picture on it and said, "Give therefore to the emperor the things that are the emperor's, and to God the things that are God's" (v. 21). Jesus' answer, which left the Pharisees "amazed," was not flippant. Nevertheless, we can accept the seriousness of the response while envisioning Jesus turning to smile at his disciples as the religious leaders walked away in a huff.

The writer of the Gospel of John records another exchange that suggests Jesus' clever wit. During a winter festival in Jerusalem, Jesus was entering the temple when a group of Jews gathered around him and began questioning him about his identity. Jesus told them, "The Father and I are one" (10:30). The Jews were outraged by what they considered to be a blasphemous response. As they picked up stones to stone Jesus, he replied, "I have shown you many good works from the Father. For which of these are you going to stone me?" (10:32). If you had been a disciple listening to this exchange, how would you have heard Jesus' words? Jesus' question about his "good works" was at least a quick-witted and ironic reply to the hostile action being considered. Could it also have been delightfully sarcastic? Can you imagine the disciples hiding smiles and stifling smirks? Can you hear them repeating Jesus' words over dinner that evening, imitating the Jewish leaders' reactions and laughing out loud?

Still another scene took place during the most powerful and passionate week in Jesus' life, yet we see that Jesus had not lost his sense of humor. The crowds were spreading branches as Jesus rode the donkey along the path into Jerusalem. Though Jesus was aware of what lay ahead, at the moment he was part of a grand celebration. We read that "the whole multitude of the disciples began to praise God joyfully with a loud voice for all the deeds of power that they had seen" (Luke 19:37). The Pharisees, who were greatly distressed and angered by all they saw and heard, said to Jesus, "Teacher, order your disciples to stop" (v. 39). Jesus replied, "I tell you, if these were silent, the stones would shout

out" (v. 40). Perhaps Jesus had a slight, knowing smile as once again he got the best of the Pharisees.

As these and other gospel accounts suggest, Jesus tended his mind by using his quick wit. With attentive listening, lightning-like responses, and perfect timing, he bested his opponents with comebacks and one-liners that were no doubt repeated many times by his followers with great pleasure and amusement. Jesus certainly was not trying to provide entertainment; his mission and his ministry were very serious business. Even so, having a sense of humor and being able to laugh were not contrary to that purpose. Finding humor and delight in the events of the day must have been healthy medicine for Jesus and his disciples.

Perhaps if we allow the possibility that Jesus used his wit during an otherwise harsh and bitter exchange, we, too, can learn how to diffuse tense, angry, or bitter situations. We may find that using a bit of wit or a touch of humor can disarm both sides in an argument. And if we allow the possibility that Jesus laughed with his disciples, we may find him more approachable ourselves. Then, as we hear him laugh, perhaps we can relax a little, sit down beside him, and listen to his next story.

"My Father Is Still Working"

After this there was a festival of the Jews, and Jesus went up to Jerusalem.

Now in Jerusalem by the Sheep Gate there is a pool, called in Hebrew Beth-zatha, which has five porticoes. In these lay many invalids—blind, lame, and paralyzed. One man was there who had been ill for thirty-eight years. When Jesus saw him lying there and knew that he had been there a long time, he said to him, "Do you want to be made well?" The sick man answered him, "Sir, I have no one to put me into the pool when the water is stirred up; and while I am making my way, someone else steps down ahead of me." Jesus said to him, "Stand up, take your mat and walk." At once the man was made well, and he took up his mat and began to walk.

Now that day was a sabbath. So the Jews said to the man who had been cured, "It is the sabbath; it is not lawful for you to carry your mat." But he answered them, "The man who made me well said to me, 'Take up your mat and walk.'" They asked him, "Who is the man who said to you, 'Take it up and walk'?" Now the man who had been healed did not know who it was, for Jesus had disappeared in the crowd that was there. Later Jesus found him in the temple and said to him, "See, you have been made well! Do not sin any more, so that nothing worse happens to you." The man went away and told the Jews that it was Jesus who had made him well. Therefore the Jews started persecuting Jesus, because he was doing such things on the sabbath. But Jesus answered them, "My Father is still working, and I also am working." For this reason the Jews were seeking all the more to kill him, because he was not only breaking the sabbath, but was also calling God his own Father, thereby making himself equal to God. (John 5:1-18)

This story, found only in the Gospel of John, is similar to many other gospel stories in which Jesus heals someone and then is criticized by the Jewish religious leaders. A man, lying in a portico near a pool of water, has been ill and unable to walk for thirty-eight years. Jesus enters the area, sees the man, and goes to him. The lame man does not know Jesus—neither his name nor his reputation. After asking the man whether he wants to be made well, Jesus heals him, saying, "Stand up, take your mat and walk" (5:8).

Imagine the rest of the story being performed by a group of comic actors. Watch the stage as the next three scenes unfold. The man who has been healed is walking across the stage, carrying his mat and rejoicing at his good fortune. The Jewish religious leaders enter and spot the man. With robes flying, they rush over to him, shouting. They are outraged! The man is carrying a *mat!* They upbraid the man, spelling out the charge against him. "It is the sabbath; it is not lawful for you to carry your mat."

As a member of the audience, knowing what we know, we laugh aloud at this ridiculous scene. This poor man, ill for thirty-eight years and now suddenly healed, has been caught in the act of carrying his *mat!* Innocently, the man recounts the events leading to this unlawful act. "The man who made me well said to me, 'Take up your mat and walk'" (5:11). The religious leader repeats the phrase about the mat as he asks the identity of this healer. Both the actor playing the healed man and the one playing the Jewish authority emphasize the mat. How funny—and ridiculous—the reenactment becomes as the religious leaders flap their robes and wring their hands in comic horror about this serious offense. "The mat, the mat, he is carrying the mat!"

In the next brief scene in our play, Jesus finds the man in the temple and speaks with him again. Learning the identity of his healer, the man returns to tell the religious leaders. Again speaking innocently and with joy, the man says, "His name is Jesus! Jesus told me to take up my mat and walk!" The man dances around, marveling at his legs and his new strength and freedom. As the visible signs of anger among the religious leaders increase, one of the leaders slaps the mat out of the arms of the man.

In the final scene, the Jewish authorities approach Jesus. It's bad enough that Jesus caused the man to sin by telling him to carry his mat, they argue; what's worse is that Jesus "sinned" himself by healing the man in the first place. Doing such work on the Sabbath is certainly breaking the law. Jesus has heard these charges before. He gets an earful once again. Jesus knows—and the audience knows, too—that these Jewish authorities are not looking at the big picture. They are unwilling to see what really matters. A man walks after thirty-eight years, and all they can focus on is a mat. A man makes people well, makes them whole, and all they can focus on are the rules.

The Jesus actor turns toward the audience. He raises his eyebrow, almost smiles, and gives a slight shrug of his shoulders. Then he turns back to the religious leaders and says, "My Father is still working, and I also am working." Now that's a great line—understated, obvious, sarcastic, and sure to make the religious leaders look foolish. Jesus reminds them that God is still on the job, so he figures it is okay for him to work, too. The religious leaders in uncontrollable anger exit the stage, tearing their robes and shouting, "Blasphemy! He deserves to die!" Meanwhile, the healed man reappears. Jesus retrieves and carries the mat and puts his arm around the man's shoulders as the two "condemned" men walk slowly in the opposite direction.

This is a funny story, but it is bitter humor. The more traditional reading of an entirely serious event and a hostile encounter may be closer to the truth. Perhaps, however, Jesus does use his quick wit to give the religious leaders a verbal slap in the face, hoping to startle them out of their obsession over Sabbath laws just long enough to focus on the man, rather than on the mat. Jesus hopes to make them see that God's healing work is more important than rules.

Sometimes humor can transform a situation, break the tension, start some laughter, and cause people to look at their own foolishness. That does not happen this time. Jesus' choice of words, "My Father," is more offensive to the religious leaders than carrying mats or healing on the Sabbath. Jesus relates himself directly to God. This is blasphemy. The Jewish authorities think Jesus should be killed.

Though Jesus' wit does not soften and win over the religious leaders, he tends his own mind by using this gift. He knows when his opponents are beyond open-minded debate, beyond listening and reconsidering their position. Rather than getting angry or becoming exhausted by endless debate, he delivers his line and lets them go. He has the satisfaction of speaking the truth and rendering his enemies speechless. They are no match for his sharp wit. We can imagine that later in the day, Jesus hears his words repeated by his disciples and others as they retell the story to those who were not there, emphasizing the "punch line": "My Father is still working, and I also am working." Perhaps Jesus thinks and hopes, *Maybe someone will get the point. Maybe someone will think about God and God's work. Maybe someone will see beyond the mat.*

Reflection

When Jesus called his disciples, he issued a simple, straightforward invitation: "Follow me." The account in Matthew indicates that the fishermen—first Peter and Andrew, and later James and John—immediately left their nets and followed Jesus (4:18-22). They did not ask questions or stop to consider this major decision. Another would-be disciple wanted to follow Jesus but said he needed to bury his father first. Jesus gave what sounds like an impatient and heartless reply, saying, "Follow me, and let the dead bury their own dead" (Matthew 8:21-22). From these accounts, we might assume that Jesus expected, even demanded, immediate answers to important questions—particularly questions related to following him.

Jesus did not, however, always insist on snap decisions. In fact, more often he taught that one should count the cost of any major undertaking, pausing to reflect on the consequences and the future implications of one's words and actions. When calling his disciples, Jesus may have wanted an immediate decision from the heart—an emotional, passionate response based on rapport and trust. Perhaps he was looking for a gut reaction, a soul knowing, a heartfelt "Yes!" As we will see, however, Jesus generally advocated giving careful thought before taking action.

When speaking to a large crowd about being his disciple, Jesus sounded like an economist doing a cost-benefit analysis (Luke 14:25-33). He compared the decision to that of a man deciding to build a tower, who first "sit[s] down and estimate[s] the cost, to see whether he has enough to complete it" (v. 28). He also used a military example, asking, "What king, going out to wage war against another king, will not sit down first and consider whether he is able with ten thousand to oppose the one who comes against him with twenty thousand?" (v. 31). Jesus told his listeners to consider the high cost of discipleship, which, according to this text, includes "hating" one's family and life itself (v. 26), carrying the cross (v. 27), and giving away all one's possessions (v. 33). Jesus was a realist. He did not glamorize life as his follower, nor did he invite anyone to a trial run—a try-it-and-maybe-you-will-like-it kind of following. Rather, he clearly indicated that anyone considering discipleship should give it very serious thought.

One young man counted the cost of discipleship and refused it, illustrating that pausing to reflect on a decision does not always mean one will make the best decision. All three Synoptic Gospels record the encounter between Jesus and the rich, young ruler (e.g., Mark 10:17-22). Jesus asked him to give up all of his possessions, and the man walked away grieving. He counted the cost and found the price too high.

Jesus offered another economic lesson, with some application also related to reflection, as he taught his listeners not to act on short-sighted impulse but, instead, to consider investing for the future. In the Sermon on the Mount, he talked about those who hear his words and act on them versus those who hear but refuse to act on them (Matthew 7:24-27). The former are like a wise man who builds his house on rock where it can withstand the inevitable storms. The latter are like a foolish man who builds his house on sand where it will be washed away when the rain and wind come. Another example of making hasty decisions in the present without thinking about the future is found in the parable of the Bridesmaids (Matthew 25:1-13). Five of the ten bridesmaids took their lamps and rushed out to meet the bridegroom without stopping to get additional oil for the lamps. The other five took extra oil for their lamps. The first five missed out on the celebration when they ran out of oil and their lamps went dark. Of course, Jesus was not giving lessons on homebuilding or on stockpiling resources for future use. Rather, he was calling us to use our minds to reflect on the deeper meanings of his messages, such as being prepared for a lifetime of discipleship (Matthew 7) and preparing for the kingdom of heaven (Matthew 25).

Though Jesus did, indeed, say that we are to count the cost and to consider investing for the future, he did not mean that we are to be overly conservative in the present, avoiding all risks. In telling another parable with economic content, Jesus recounted the story of a master who went on a journey and gave his property to three slaves to manage (Matthew 25:14-30). Although this parable of the Talents, like the parable of the Bridesmaids, is Jesus' description of what the kingdom of heaven will be like, our focus here is on the behavior of the characters. The third slave in this telling of the parable of the Talents received one talent which he buried in the ground. His report to the master indicated that he paused to reflect on what he should do with the money entrusted to him. He said, "Master, I knew that you were a harsh man, reaping where you did not sow, and gathering where you did not scatter seed" (v. 24). Unfortunately, the slave was so afraid of making a bad investment that he took no risk at all and returned only the one talent to his master. The master was angry and called for harsh punishment.

In his own words and actions, Jesus certainly counted the cost and paused to consider the consequences. Again, this does not mean that he chose to play it safe, to avoid risk and controversy. Quite the contrary, Jesus often incurred significant cost in speaking his mind and acting his conscience. In Luke 6:6-11 we read about one of many times when Jesus healed on the Sabbath. Once again he knew that the Pharisees were watching him. The gospel writer reports further that Jesus "knew what they were thinking" (Luke 6:8). This suggests thoughtful calculation on Jesus' part about what would happen if he healed in the synagogue on the Sabbath. He did heal the man with the withered hand and, as expected, the Pharisees were "filled with fury" (Luke 6:11).

How did reflecting on decisions help Jesus to tend his mind if often his decisions led to such disastrous consequences? Perhaps it enabled him to avoid, or at least lessen, the potentially destructive emotion of regret. After all, choosing to act on impulse rather than to stop and reflect often leads to bad decisions, and constant replaying of a bad decision can lead to deep regret and, ultimately, destroy the mind.

Of course, there are times when regretting the consequences of a decision may be unavoidable or even appropriate, such as when a loved one dies in a plane crash. The decision to fly on the plane, after all, was not necessarily a bad one. There are other times, however, when regretting the consequences of a poor or hasty decision may lead to a different kind of regret—such as when someone is killed due to another individual's decision to drink and drive. This regret, due to a thoughtless and bad choice, may be totally destructive.

Although Jesus' choice to follow God led to his own suffering as well as the suffering of others, his mind knew far more peace than regret because he tended his mind well by always reflecting, considering, and counting the cost.

"Jesus Bent Down and Wrote"

Jesus went to the Mount of Olives. Early in the morning he came again to the temple. All the people came to him and he sat down and began to teach them. The scribes and the Pharisees brought a woman who had been caught in adultery; and making her stand before all of them, they said to him, "Teacher, this woman was caught in the very act of committing adultery. Now in the law Moses commanded us to stone such women. Now what do you say?" They said this to test him, so that they might have some charge to bring against him. Jesus bent down and wrote with his finger on the ground. When they kept on questioning him, he straightened up and said to them, "Let anyone among you who is without sin be the first to throw a stone at her." And once again he bent down and wrote on the ground. When they heard it, they went away, one by one, beginning with the elders; and Jesus was left alone with the woman standing before him. Jesus straightened up and said to her, "Woman, where are they? Has no one condemned you?" She said, "No one, sir." And Jesus said, "Neither do

I condemn you. Go your way, and from now on do not sin again."
(John 8:1-11)

What did Jesus write on the ground? No one knows, and does it really matter? Of course, knowing what he wrote would be interesting. Maybe he wrote some relevant part of the law. Perhaps he only doodled, making lines and shapes to pass the time. What does matter is that he was quiet. In response to the charges made against the woman and the question asked by the Pharisees, he said nothing at all. These religious leaders were once again trying to trap Jesus. What were his choices? He could tell them to release the woman, thus denying the validity of the law. If he opposed the law, the Pharisees would have evidence to use against him. Perhaps they would retort, "This man is no prophet! He is not even a respectable Jew. He does not obey the law. He stood in the temple and opposed the law of Moses!" However, if Jesus agreed with the Pharisees and condemned the woman to stoning, he would be violating God's higher law of love and might lose the support of many of his followers. We can imagine their critical response: "That famous teacher, that supposedly compassionate healer, allowed the Pharisees to condemn that poor woman. Why didn't he protect her? Where was the man who was involved? Is this Jesus just like the rest of them, caring only that the woman be punished?" How would Jesus respond?

Jesus paused to reflect on what he would say. Without answering their questions, he bent down to the ground and began to write in the dirt. Jesus was wise and mentally quick. The text suggests that only a brief moment of silence passed. The moment, however, was crucially important. Jesus knew a woman's life was at stake—as well as his own reputation. Furthermore, all the people gathered in the temple would hear his response, see the woman's and the Pharisees' reactions, and take this experience home with them. They would tell others, and all would discuss the event and learn something from it. During that pause, Jesus, in effect, removed himself from the crowd. He withdrew—bent down without any eye contact, without any response.

After considering what he would say, Jesus stood up and gave a brilliant response: "Let anyone among you who is without sin be the first to throw a stone at her" (v. 7). He did not condemn her according to the law.

He did not dismiss the law and tell the Pharisees to release her immediately. Neither did he find some middle-ground compromise, such as
accepting her guilt while trying to negotiate a reduced punishment.
Such a compromise might have satisfied everyone, or no one. No, Jesus
chose a radically different direction. He turned the focus
on the woman's accusers, putting them in the difficult and awkward
position of having to choose between two undesirable choices. If they
threw a stone, they would be declaring themselves without sin. They
knew that only God is without sin. To equate themselves with God
would be blasphemous (as they were very quick to tell Jesus when he
made that claim!). However, if they backed down on their accusation
and the punishment set in the law, they would not only look foolish but
also set a bad precedent before the crowd—forgiveness, no less!

Jesus' next action was as important as the previous one. Again, he
bent down to the ground and began to write. Once again he paused.
This time he might have been wondering what the Pharisees would do.
From what we read elsewhere in the Gospels, we might be reluctant to
assume that they would make the right choice. As they often did, they
could have ignored Jesus' words or manipulated them to mean something else. They could have thrown him out of the temple and continued with their duty of enforcing the law. Perhaps if Jesus had moved
closer to the accusers and stood eye to eye, the Pharisees might have
felt pressured and responded with angry words and actions. Instead, by
bending down and being quiet, Jesus left the Pharisees alone, each with
his own conscience. The silence must have been disarming.

Jesus' pause allowed each man to reflect on his own sin. The elders
left first. The gospel writer includes that significant piece of the story.
The ones who were most thoughtful and wise realized first that they
could be—should be—standing alongside the woman accused of sin.
They had the courage and character to look at themselves and admit
their failings. Finally, all the accusers left. Jesus did not condemn the
woman but sent her on her way, saying, "Do not sin again" (v. 11).

Jesus tended his mind by pausing to reflect before answering important questions or making significant decisions. He was not indecisive,
unable to move past the silence to speak. Rather, he was appropriately
careful and thoughtful. On other occasions recorded in the Gospels, he
responded to a question with a question of his own, often asking, "What

do you think?" Although this technique gave him time to reflect on his own answer, Jesus more likely used the technique to reveal what was underneath the original question posed to him and to make the questioner reflect. This time, after delivering his wise and challenging directive to the Pharisees, he used silence. What a powerful silence it was.

Openness

The gospel accounts show us that Jesus made decisions after careful thought and reflection. Although he talked about the importance of counting the cost, he did not say that every decision should be final. He challenged long-held practices and beliefs, calling for people to change their minds and their ways. By the time he began his preaching and teaching ministry, Jesus had reconsidered and reinterpreted what he had been taught about Scripture. He had views about what the law required that were contrary to what was being taught and practiced by most of the religious leaders. He had opened his mind to view people as children of God instead of as clean or unclean. Jesus tended his mind by being open to ideas, perspectives, and values that sometimes opposed accepted teaching but always focused on God and God's love.

In his preaching, Jesus often reinterpreted parts of the law. In one section of the Sermon on the Mount, for example, six times Jesus introduced a teaching with the phrase (or part of the phrase), "You have heard that it was said . . . but I say to you" (Matthew 5:21-48). First he quoted the law, and then he explained his reinterpretation. At other times he challenged the religious leaders to reconsider their understanding and practice of the law (e.g., Matthew 15:1-20). Jesus' own actions indicated that he had different ideas about the rules regarding cleanliness, including who was considered clean and acceptable and who was not. Jesus talked to Samaritan women, touched lepers, visited in areas where Gentiles lived, and talked with and touched persons possessed by demons. In these and other ways, Jesus tried to get others to let go of prejudices and change their minds about what they believed.

Did Jesus change his mind frequently during his ministry? The gospel accounts do not record Jesus making choices on major decisions and later changing his mind. On the other hand, Jesus surely was not rigid and inflexible in his thinking. He engaged in open dialogue with his disciples and listened to their ideas and opinions. It is likely, then, that he may have changed his mind about some things. Consider, for example, his encounter with the Canaanite woman who asked him to heal her daughter. At first he did not respond (Matthew 15:21-28). When the woman continued her pleading, he explained why he was not willing to heal a Canaanite. Finally, Jesus seemed to change his mind when he acknowledged the woman's faith and healed her daughter. Here, Jesus showed his willingness to reconsider his own assumptions. In other encounters and in his teaching and preaching, Jesus indicated his desire for others to open their minds. Again and again he encouraged individuals to change their minds and their hearts.

One day Jesus was teaching in the temple when he told a parable about two sons (Matthew 21:28-32). The father asked the first son to go in his vineyard and work. The son said that he would not go. Later "he changed his mind and went" (v. 29). The father also asked the same of the second son, who responded that he would go and work in the vineyard. This son, however, did not go. Jesus asked, "Which of the two did the will of his father?" (v. 31). Those listening replied that the first son had done his father's will. Jesus was emphasizing the importance of what one does over what one says. Making a promise is of no value if it is not kept. The son who changed his mind ultimately did the right thing. Perhaps it would have been better if he had cheerfully said, "Yes, I will be glad to go and work in the vineyard," and then had gone. Yet he reconsidered his negative response. He probably thought about his father, the work that needed to be done, his responsibility in the family, and his attitude; and he changed his mind. Although the virtue of changing one's mind is not the main point, the parable does illustrate the value of reconsidering.

After telling the parable of the Two Sons, Jesus continued to address his listeners, including the chief priests and the elders who had questioned him. He told them that the tax collectors and the prostitutes would enter the kingdom of God ahead of them because these "sinners" believed in John (Matthew 21:31-32). To the religious leaders he said, "Even after you saw it, you did not change your minds and believe him" (v. 32). Throughout Jesus' ministry, most of the Pharisees and other Jewish leaders were unwilling to change their minds, holding fast to their own interpretation of the law. They spent their time looking for ways to trap Jesus rather than considering the new ideas that he was offering to them.

In another parable about two sons, Jesus told of the younger son, the "prodigal," who decided to take his inheritance and leave home (Luke 15:11-32). The young man lost everything he owned and ended up feeding pigs in a field. His thought process of reconsidering and changing his mind is described by Jesus: "But when he came to himself he said, 'How many of my father's hired hands have bread enough and to spare, but here I am dying of hunger! I will get up and go to my father'" (vv. 17-18). After thinking about his situation and his options, he swallowed whatever was left of his pride to face the potentially humiliating prospect of returning home. Changing one's mind can be difficult because it sometimes requires admitting that what was previously said, believed, or done was wrong. This young man was greatly rewarded for reconsidering the direction of his life.

Although the fate of the prodigal was far better than he had hoped, that of another man in the gospel accounts who changed his mind is worse than he ever imagined. Judas, when he realized the consequences of his choice, returned to the chief priests and the elders who had paid him to betray Jesus and said, "I have sinned by betraying innocent blood" (Matthew 27:4). The religious leaders, who had what they wanted now that Jesus had been arrested, had no interest in Judas's change of mind. Judas could not undo what he had done, nor could he live with the result of his choice. Although the willingness and ability to reconsider decisions—to consider new information, admit past errors, and change one's mind—can be a virtue, Judas's experience demonstrates that reconsidering decisions cannot always make everything right. Major decisions need careful thought before they are made. Changing one's mind later may be an option, but trying to reverse an earlier decision can be costly.

Stubborn refusal to let go of what we have always thought, regardless of the evidence to the contrary, does not tend our minds well. A healthy, well-tended mind displays openness to new ideas and a willingness to reconsider long-held beliefs and habits. Jesus valued open minds. Only a person with both an open mind and an open heart would receive the good news and choose to follow him.

"In No One in Israel Have I Found Such Faith"

When he entered Capernaum, a centurion came to him, appealing to him and saying, "Lord, my servant is lying at home paralyzed, in ter-

rible distress." And he said to him, "I will come and cure him." The centurion answered, "Lord, I am not worthy to have you come under my roof; but only speak the word, and my servant will be healed. For I also am a man under authority, with soldiers under me; and I say to one, 'Go,' and he goes, and to another, 'Come,' and he comes, and to my slave, 'Do this,' and the slave does it." When Jesus heard him, he was amazed and said to those who followed him, "Truly I tell you, in no one in Israel have I found such faith. I tell you, many will come from east and west and will eat with Abraham and Isaac and Jacob in the kingdom of heaven, while the heirs of the kingdom will be thrown into the outer darkness, where there will be weeping and gnashing of teeth." And to the centurion Jesus said, "Go; let it be done for you according to your faith." And the servant was healed in that hour. (Matthew 8:5-13)

More than once, Jesus declared that his ministry was among the Jews, saying, "I was sent only to the lost sheep of the house of Israel" (Matthew 15:24). Earlier, when sending out his twelve disciples as missionaries, Jesus gave them the same direction concerning those to whom they should minister: "Go nowhere among the Gentiles, and enter no town of the Samaritans, but go rather to the lost sheep of the house of Israel" (Matthew 10:5-6). Jesus' words are clear. His understanding, as presented in Matthew's Gospel, was that God had sent him to preach, teach, and heal among the Jews. Look, however, at Jesus' ministry.

To the centurion asking that his servant be healed, Jesus commended the man's faith. In fact, Jesus said that the man's faith exceeded that of others he had encountered among the Jews.

On another occasion, Jesus first told a Canaanite woman that she was not among those to whom he had been called to minister. After she argued with him that even dogs get the leftovers from the table and, therefore, even a Gentile woman such as herself deserved something from him, Jesus responded, "Woman, great is your faith! Let it be done for you as you wish" (Matthew 15:28). Then he healed the woman's daughter.

Another time, Jesus was on his way to Jerusalem when ten lepers approached him. Jesus sent them to the priests who could declare them clean, and they were healed on the way. Only one, a Samaritan, returned to Jesus to thank him. After asking about the others, Jesus said to this one, "Get up and go on your way; your faith has made you well" (Luke 17:19).

To another Samaritan, the woman at Jacob's well, Jesus discussed heritage and faith. She believed he was the Messiah and became a missionary among the Samaritans.

On yet another day, when telling a parable about being a neighbor, Jesus chose a Samaritan as the exemplary neighbor. Two Jews—one a priest—were actually depicted as the men who failed to love others as the law required.

If Jesus thought that he was called to minister among the Jews, why did he teach and heal among these Gentiles? Did he change his mind about his calling? No, Jesus never abandoned his mission among the Jews. He was, however, willing to acknowledge faith and accept people of faith whoever they were and wherever he found them. Jesus extended his compassion to Gentiles who were willing to receive the gifts of healing, inclusion, and love that he offered.

Among the Jews, Jesus accepted those who were labeled unacceptable by the religious authorities. He seemed to look right into a person's heart and soul. One's health, background, profession, and even behavior did not give Jesus pause if the person was open to him and his message. Jesus' openness and acceptance, however, were not merely some blanket "God loves you" offered from a distance. He had regular fellowship with those who were labeled "sinners" and even called a despised tax collector to be one of his disciples. As he did among the Gentiles, Jesus found faith and extended his compassion among the "unclean" Jews. This is why Jesus was often criticized for associating with persons whom the Jewish leaders claimed should be excluded from the fellowship of the community of faith.

Jesus also was open to denouncing those who rejected him—those who self-righteously claimed to be recipients of God's favor while excluding others from the community. The Jewish religious leaders who abused their position and power were consistently the object of Jesus' accusations. Jesus said to them, "But woe to you, scribes and Pharisees, hypocrites! For you lock people out of the kingdom of heaven. For you do not go in yourselves, and when others are going in, you stop them" (Matthew 23:13).

Jesus did not start out with a set of assumptions or rules about which people were acceptable to God. He had an open mind and listened to people. He perceived and cared about what was in a person's heart. As a result, he could affirm the faith of the centurion and of the Canaanite woman. Likewise, he could tell the priests that they were not righteous and did not know Scripture or the God of love.

Jesus tended his mind well by keeping it open to the unexpected. Being open, however, was more than a mental exercise. To an open mind, he added an open heart. He opened his mind and his heart when and where it counted: accepting persons based on what matters most. Jesus did not change his mind about being sent to the lost sheep of Israel. He did, however, use his mind and his heart to look critically at the sheep. He welcomed rejected lambs to his pasture and pointed established sheep toward the gate.

Questions for Reflection and Discussion

1. Choose one of the following activities to give your mind some exercise.
   a) Choose a favorite parable of Jesus. Rewrite or retell the parable using a contemporary setting and circumstances. How does updating the parable affect its meaning for you?
   b) Read carefully one of the four gospels, perhaps reading one chapter each day. Choose one verse from that chapter to reflect on throughout the day.
   c) Select two or three significant events in Jesus' life that are recorded in several of the Gospels. For each event, read the account in each Gospel where it is found. Notice all the similarities and differences among the various accounts. Think about why each gospel writer may have wanted to include particular details.
2. The Pharisees exercised their minds—actively studying the law and imposing it rigidly on others—without balancing their thoughts and actions with compassion from their hearts. Have you been in a position of authority—parent, teacher, committee chair, boss—and used your mind to impose rules and make evaluations without any balance from your heart? Or, have you let your heart rule your decisions without thoughtful guidance

from your mind? In either case, what were the results of your decisions and actions, and how might you provide better balance in this area of your life?

3. What are some things we often worry about? What two or three things do you worry about most? Jesus lessened the possibility of worry capturing his own mind by simplifying his life, meeting troubling challenges head on, and sharing his burdens with his disciples and with God. Apply these practices that Jesus followed to make a plan for dealing with at least one of your worries.

4. Jesus said, "Do not be anxious"; instead, "look at the birds" and "consider the lilies." Jesus was pointing out God's care for creation—providing food for birds, who do not plant, and "clothes" for flowers, which do not sew. What other images come to mind that illustrate this concept of God's care? Choose your own image and write a phrase to convey it. Use your image to help you rest your mind by: (1) focusing on the outside world rather than your worries, (2) gaining perspective and remembering what really matters, and (3) meditating on God's creation. Share your image with someone else.

5. Worry is not the only obstacle to resting our minds. Long hours of work (whether paid or unpaid) without a break can exhaust both body and mind. Do you take adequate breaks from work on a daily and weekly basis? If so, when do you make time for breaks, and what do you do to refresh and renew yourself? If you do not take adequate breaks from your work, what prevents you from doing so?

6. Traditionally, pictures of Jesus have not depicted him with a smile on his face, much less laughing—though some contemporary artists are working to change this. Can you recall an occasion in Jesus' life when you think he might have laughed? What makes you laugh? What are three ways you can tend your heart with laughter? Practice each one during the coming week, remembering that laughter is good for both the physical heart and the emotional heart.

7. The rich, young ruler counted the cost of discipleship and decided that the cost was too high. Why do you believe some

members of our society view church membership as a beneficial "credential" with little, if any, cost? Do you believe we can be true disciples if we perceive little or no cost to our discipleship? Why or why not? What are the personal costs to you in choosing to be a disciple of Jesus?

8. Jesus counted the cost of following God's call. The costs were high indeed: suffering and death. Nevertheless, Jesus kept following, walking. Can you recall a time in your faith journey when you were faced with a costly decision? What did you decide and why? Did family and friends support or oppose you in your decision? In hindsight, what were the effects of that decision in your life? How do you feel about that decision now?

9. Jesus may have been surprised to find such strong faith in the centurion and the Canaanite woman. Clearly he was disappointed in the Jewish religious leaders' lack of faith. Whatever preconceived notions—prejudices—he may have had about Gentiles and Jewish religious leaders, he let go of them in light of his experience. What prejudices do you find in yourself or recognize in our society? What keeps us from examining our prejudices about certain groups? What effects may prejudice have on the heart of the person making the judgment? on the person against whom the prejudice is directed?

4. Tending the Soul

WHAT IS THE SOUL? THE WORD MAY ELICIT A THOUGHT, OR PERHAPS just a feeling, of something deep within and vital. Yet we can search using any technology and fail to locate the soul. No one definition clarifies or satisfies. Defining the body is easy, as is identifying the mind. Explaining the heart in a context other than the blood-pumping organ is more challenging. Defining and explaining the soul may be the most difficult of all. The word *soul* is used in many different ways. It can bring to mind soul music or a poet with soul or a performance that lacks soul. Soul as descriptive of part of our being, however, is not quite the same. How, then, can we tend something we cannot locate and do not understand?

What do we read about the soul in Scripture? In Hebrew Scripture, the soul, often partnered with the heart, is the part of our being called to respond to God. Perhaps the most familiar verse, the one repeated by Jesus as the greatest commandment, is found in Deuteronomy 6:5: "You shall love the LORD your God with all your heart, and with all your soul, and with all your might." The phrase "with all your heart and with all your soul" is used throughout Deuteronomy to describe how we are to search for God (4:29), serve God (10:12), observe the statutes and ordinances (26:16), obey God (30:2), and turn to God (30:10). The psalmist also speaks frequently of the soul. For example, the soul rejoices (16:9), praises (30:12), and waits for the Lord (33:20). The soul is described vividly throughout Psalm 42, beginning with the soul's longing and thirsting for God. Clearly, the soul is the part of our being that relates to God.

Jesus said that we are not to be afraid of persons who can destroy the body but not the soul; rather, we are to fear only the one who can destroy both (Matthew 10:28). This verse suggests that the soul is separate from and unlike the body. Although Jesus' words indicate that no human action can destroy our soul, he did not define precisely the soul or explain how it is separate from the body. The task here is not to argue one particular meaning of the soul. The word *soul* is familiar even if not fully understood. This aspect of our being, often identified with our spiritual nature, needs tending in ways other than those we've considered for the body, heart, and mind. For our purposes here, let us think of the soul as the part of our being that hears the voice of God, experiences the presence of God, and knows God. The soul is our deepest place, the very core, the essence of our being. It reflects the image of God within each of us, which is revealed as we seek to be the persons God has created and called us to be.

How, then, did Jesus tend his soul, the essence of whom God created and called him to be? In the reflections that follow, we will see that he spent time appreciating nature, the wonders of God's glorious creation. We will consider how Jesus' experience of God in and through nature had seemingly contradictory effects. At times he was filled with the beauty and rhythms of creation, which drew him close to God. At other times and in other places, he was emptied and tested through the starkness of creation, experiencing perhaps a keener sense of his reliance on God. We also will see that Jesus tended his soul by practicing forgiveness and by teaching others to forgive, by spending time in prayer, and by following what he understood to be God's call—God's path for his life. This following was the ultimate goal for which all the other tending was necessary. If we follow Jesus, tending our souls as we see him tend his, we will be on the path toward health and wholeness in body, heart, mind, and soul.

Nature

According to the account in Matthew, Jesus was born in Bethlehem. He lived briefly in Egypt and grew up in Nazareth. As an adult, Jesus went to be baptized by John, who had been preaching in Judea near the Jordan River. A brief review of these locations on a map indicates that Jesus was familiar with much of Galilee, Judea, and the surrounding territory. Why, then, did Jesus choose to settle in Capernaum? Jesus may have had several good reasons, none of which are known to us with any certainty. We may speculate, however, that Matthew gives us a clue to one possible reason: "He left Nazareth and made his home in Capernaum by the sea" (Matthew 4:13). The phrase "by the sea" may be one key to the attraction of Capernaum. Of course, the sea provided the practical advantage of facilitating transportation in the region. The fishing industry and related commerce may have offered additional advantages to Jesus. At the very least, the industry yielded several of his better-known disciples! The appeal of the sea, however, goes beyond practical concerns.

If we were to look up the words *sea* and *mountain* in a Bible concordance and read all the gospel references, we would see that Jesus experienced each of these locations numerous times. Jesus could have stayed in the city—whether Capernaum or Jerusalem or elsewhere—but he chose frequently to walk by the sea, to be in a boat on the sea, and to climb up a mountain. In the Gospel of Mark, for example, we read: "Jesus departed with his disciples to the sea, and a great multitude from Galilee followed him" (3:7), and "[Jesus] went up the mountain and called to him those whom he wanted, and they came to him" (3:13). Likewise, we read in the Gospel of Matthew, "After Jesus had left [the district of Tyre and Sidon], he passed along the Sea of Galilee, and he went up the mountain, where he sat down" (15:29).

Why did Jesus move to these natural settings to preach and to teach? Why, when he needed time alone, did he usually go to the sea or a mountain? Most of us can answer these questions based on our own experience. Being in a natural environment where we can breathe fresh air, see trees, and hear birds—whether just outside our back door or miles away from home—can heighten our senses and our awareness of the Creator. If the scenery is particularly dramatic and beautiful, we may be opened to an unusual sense of God's presence. So, too, Jesus sometimes met crowds by the sea or on a mountain to draw them closer to the Creator and to focus them on his message. When he needed quiet time for his own soul, frequently he escaped from the crowd to places where God could speak in and through nature.

The Gospels reveal that Jesus appreciated other aspects of nature as well. Despite the traditional belief that his father Joseph was a carpenter, not a farmer, Jesus was unusually attentive to the surrounding agrarian culture. Many of his parables and teachings demonstrate that he was a careful observer of agriculture. The fact that he was attuned to the rhythms of the seasons and of planting and harvesting is evident in the parable of the Sower (Matthew 13:3-8). One can imagine that Jesus watched as birds ate the seeds on the path, as young plants withered in the rocky soil, and as weeds choked out other sprouting plants. In another example, a parable about wheat and weeds, Jesus revealed some knowledge of farming practices (Matthew 13:24-30). His listeners would have known about the practice of letting the weeds remain until the harvest. Jesus needed to know, too, lest any mistake in describing farming methods distract the people from his message about the kingdom of heaven.

Jesus was a masterful teacher. He talked about seeds, planting, vineyards, wheat harvests, birds, flowers, and the color of the sky—all of which connected with the interests and experiences of his listeners. His awareness, knowledge, and experience of these things also connected him to God. Noticing the details of and changes in God's creation, after all, is a form of response to God.

How might nature touch and tend the soul of Jesus? We can consider how nature has touched our own souls and imagine similar experiences in Jesus. Being surrounded by nature may draw us close to God in intimate and mysterious ways. Picture the ocean, for example. The power of the ocean may speak to us of the power of God. A beach littered with shells, all different, may remind us of the infinite diversity of God's creation. A snowy egret, delicate and quiet at the edge of a marsh, may alert us to the still, small voice of God. A baby loggerhead turtle may cause us to smile with delight and to reflect on the struggle and the hope of life in God's world. Similar soul experiences can be found on a mountain, in a flower garden, in a storm, or in a vineyard.

By the sea, on the sea, up a mountain, and in fields and gardens, Jesus spent time with God's moving and powerful creations. As he carefully observed nature, he tended his own soul. His example is an invitation for us to do the same.

"Look at the Fig Tree"

Then he told them a parable: "Look at the fig tree and all the trees; as soon as they sprout leaves you can see for yourselves and know that summer is already near. So also, when you see these things taking place, you know that the kingdom of God is near." (Luke 21:29-31)

On several occasions, Jesus talked about signs. At times, religious leaders or others in a crowd demanded a sign from Jesus to prove who he was, what he claimed, and what he could do. At other times, as in Luke 21:5-28—the context for the passage above—Jesus described signs of the coming of the kingdom of God. Here his disciples, and others who were listening, were no doubt alarmed and frightened by Jesus' descriptions of the events surrounding the arrival of the kingdom. They asked Jesus several questions: "When will this happen and what will signal this coming?" Jesus told this brief parable about the fig tree to illustrate what he had already said in other ways. "There will be signs," he said.

Searching for signs of the coming of the kingdom is a popular study and activity in our culture. We can, however, find meaning in this simple statement about the fig tree, as well as in other words of Jesus about signs, without relating it to warnings about a cataclysmic end of times. Unlike many parables of Jesus that tell a story focusing on characters whose behavior reveals some lesson, here Jesus focuses on a common occurrence in nature. Within the parable itself, he gives specific instruction: "Look . . . see . . . know." If we follow these instructions as Jesus himself did, we can learn something about tending the soul.

"Look at the fig tree and all the trees" (v. 29). "*Look.*" The call is not for a one-time glance only. We will need to look at the trees carefully and often to notice the fine detail described here. Then Jesus said to "see for yourselves" (v. 30). What are we to see when we look at the trees? *See* the very first sprouting of leaves. When our searching reveals a sprout, we are seeing a sign. In this case, the meaning of the sign is clear—for us as it was for Jesus' listeners. We *know* that summer is near.

Jesus talked elsewhere about looking at nature. He said, "Look at the birds of the air" (Matthew 6:26), and, "Consider the lilies" (Matthew 6:28). He said that we are to see that the birds do not plant food, yet they eat, and that the flowers do not sew, yet they are beautifully clothed. Although he did not say so explicitly, he implied that the birds and the lilies are signs. From them we know of God's certain care for us.

Jesus accused the Pharisees and Sadducees of following closely the signs in nature while refusing to see the signs that pointed them to belief in him. He said, "When it is evening, you say, 'It will be fair weather, for the sky is red.' And in the morning, 'It will be stormy today, for the sky is red and threatening.' You know how to interpret the appearance of the sky, but you cannot interpret the signs of the times" (Matthew 16:2-3). Look at nature. See the signs. Know what the signs mean.

Fishermen and sailors may still consult the sky for weather information. Farmers may consult sprouting trees to make planting decisions. Florists may consider the beautiful "clothes" of the flowers. Those for whom bird watching is a hobby may carefully observe the habits of birds. But what if we have no professional relationship to nature or no hobby connecting us to nature; is looking for signs of any use to us? And even if we *do* notice the signs in nature, do we allow the signs to connect us to God?

Consider for a moment a different example of looking for signs. Parents may spend considerable time and energy trying to read signs from their baby. A baby gives various signs—crying is a significant one—when hungry or sleepy, for example. Parents want to respond appropriately with what is needed, but they are responding already by the act of trying to read the signs. Although this observation is not a sufficient response to the baby's needs, being attentive by watching, listening, and noticing expressions, sounds, and movements are all important responses to the baby. Similarly, taking time to notice and appreciate the sky, birds, leaves, and flowers is a response to God. By these actions we are saying that we are aware of and thankful for what God is doing in nature. If we take a little longer to sit with and meditate on the beauty and wonders of nature, we may experience the presence of God.

Look. See. Know. The rhythms of nature—the predictable cycle of spring sprouts and summer leaves—are a connection to God. Spending intimate time with nature tends our soul by drawing us closer to God. Look at the oak and maple and all the trees. As soon as they sprout leaves—or blaze with red and orange leaves, or drop their leaves—we can see the sign and know that God is near.

Wilderness

For many of us, the desert or wilderness is stark, bleak, and uninviting. It may even be threatening and dangerous. When we think about spending time in nature—in God's creation—we usually do not think of the desert or wilderness. Beaches and oceans, mountains and forests may be places where we feel close to God and hear God's voice. We may be comforted, inspired, and filled with the presence of God in these beautiful places. Our souls are tended there. Why would we ever venture into the wilderness? What benefit could such an experience provide?

In the wilderness, we may feel totally alone. The challenge of the harsh environment may confront us with our vulnerabilities, exposing our hiding places deep inside. It may empty us of all that provides our false sense of protection and security—all that separates us from total availability to God. The desert may be a place of testing for us. It was so for Jesus.

Each of the Synoptic Gospels includes an account of Jesus' time in the wilderness, after his baptism and before beginning his public ministry (Matthew 4:1-11; Mark 1:12-13; Luke 4:1-13). The writers of Matthew and Luke say that Jesus was "led" by the Spirit into the wilderness (Matthew 4:1; Luke 4:1). Mark reports more dramatically that the Spirit "drove him out into the wilderness" (Mark 1:12). Perhaps Jesus was not any more excited about this experience than we would have been! No doubt he knew, however, that this time of testing and preparation was necessary. Whether led or pushed by the Spirit of God, he did what he felt called to do. We, too, must try to do the same when we are so clearly led by the Spirit. While the pull of an early morning walk beside the ocean or along a mountain trail may be an attractive opportunity for reflection and time with God, hearing the call to go to the wilderness may require intentional openness and persistent willingness. Even then, we may need a clear push of the Spirit to move us to such a place.

The first thing Jesus did when he arrived in the wilderness was to begin a time of fasting. For forty days and nights, according to the account in Luke, he did not eat. Being alone in the wilderness and fasting were, no doubt, experiences that challenged and tested Jesus' strength and endurance. Perhaps these experiences pushed him beyond his own physical strength and ability so that his reliance had to be on God.

The Jewish practice of fasting was typically part of a religious observance accompanied by repentance and prayer. During his ministry, Jesus criticized those who made a show of their fasting, those who wanted to appear to be sacrificing so that others would notice and be impressed. Trying to get the praise of others is the opposite of the purpose of fasting, which is intended to empty one of self-absorption and the desire to receive the approval and praise of others. During a fast, the soul may be tended by harsh and difficult experiences that clean out all the ugly, hidden places. Any intentional experience with God in the wilderness, whether with fasting or not, may help the soul to find its strength to face the most difficult challenges in life, including temptations.

Jesus was famished and physically weakened by his fast but stronger in heart, mind, and soul. He was ready to face the devil, who came to tempt him. Satan tempted Jesus three times, offering everything from bread to authority over the world. Each time Jesus resisted, responding to Satan from Scripture. At the end of the exchanges with Jesus, the devil left. According to the writers of Matthew and Mark, angels came to minister to Jesus. Though we cannot know exactly what that means, the need for angels suggests that a time of testing in the wilderness can leave one so depleted—in body, heart, mind, and soul—that extraordinary care is needed.

At other times in his ministry, Jesus returned to deserted places (e.g., Luke 4:42; 5:16). Sometimes after preaching and teaching to large crowds and healing many sick and disabled persons, Jesus would get on a boat or go up a mountain with his disciples. At other times, he escaped alone to a deserted place. His soul needed tending in different ways at different times. Although the gospel accounts do not make specific reference to other temptations, surely the time in the wilderness before his ministry began was not the only time he was tempted. Perhaps the demands of more people to heal, stronger demons to exorcise, and harsher criticism from his opponents tempted him to doubt his ministry and consider giving up. Perhaps the growing crowds tempted him to use his popularity and power for personal gain. Whatever temptations or challenges he faced, the stark environment of the desert may have been the place where Jesus found strength to expose and resist these temptations and challenges.

How do we tend our own souls in the wilderness? Must we physically put ourselves in the middle of a desert? Must we go to a wilderness area with a group for physical and mental testing of our strength, self-reliance, confidence, trust, and loyalty? Well, no and yes. The soulful wilderness experience is not about learning to rely on ourselves or to trust some other person. It is, however, an intentional, and perhaps difficult, spiritual challenge meant to rid ourselves of protective barriers and self-reliance so that we may find our security in God alone. Certainly an actual desert or wilderness is not required. An environment different from our usual one—and perhaps a relatively stark place—is needed. We may not need to fast, but we may need to change what we eat. We may need to get up earlier, or stay up later to pray. We may need to spend more time walking or more time kneeling. Most of all, we simply need some time alone.

Jesus tended his soul by following the Spirit into the wilderness. Unfortunately, too many of our "religious experiences" are designed to do just the opposite. Isn't the goal of our churches and even our retreat centers to make us feel comfortable and comforted, to help us feel protected and safe? Look at Jesus and the intentional and significant times he spent in the wilderness, in deserted places. May his example give us courage and lead us to find our own deserted places to tend our souls.

"Here in the Desert"

In those days when there was again a great crowd without anything to eat, he called his disciples and said to them, "I have compassion for the crowd, because they have been with me now for three days and have nothing to eat. If I send them away hungry to their homes, they will faint on the way—and some of them have come from a great distance." His disciples replied, "How can one feed these people with bread here in the desert?" He asked them, "How many loaves do you have?" They said, "Seven." Then he ordered the crowd to sit down on the ground; and he took the seven loaves, and after giving thanks he broke them and gave them to his disciples to distribute; and they distributed them to the crowd. They had also a few small fish; and after blessing them, he ordered that these too should be distributed. They ate and were filled; and they took up the broken pieces left over, seven baskets full. Now there were about four thousand people. And he sent them away. And immediately he got into the boat with his disciples and went to the district of Dalmanutha. (Mark 8:1-10)

When John the Baptist first appeared on the scene, he was in the wilderness preaching what might be described as "hellfire and brimstone." His clothes and habits—wearing camel's hair and eating locusts—presented a "wild" picture of this man in the wilderness. After being baptized, Jesus, too, was in the wilderness for his time of testing. This was a rather "wild" event relative to most of our experiences. Forty days of fasting and having conversations with the devil in the wilderness may be unsettling for us to consider. If we think, however, that these "wild" times in the wilderness were limited to the time before Jesus began preaching and teaching, we need to take a closer look at the Gospels.

Although the word *wilderness* is not used in the Gospels to identify the setting for Jesus' ministry, the word *desert* is a label used for the same terrain. Whether described as wilderness or desert, the area referred to in the text is barren and uninviting, with wild animals and little vegetation. Jesus did not have to go far to be in such a place. Much of the area just outside the towns where he lived and preached, as well as much of the land through which he traveled, could be described as wilderness or desert. Jesus tended his soul in these areas, not only during the forty days of testing but also throughout his ministry. Often Jesus withdrew to these "deserted places." In fact, John the Baptist was not the only one preaching in the desert. In the passage above, Jesus was preaching there as well.

In both gospel accounts of Jesus feeding four thousand (Matthew 15:32-39; Mark 8:1-10), and in three of the four accounts of Jesus feeding five thousand (Matthew 14:13-21; Mark 6:30-44; and Luke 9:10-17), the setting is described as the desert or a deserted place. That Jesus fed the people in these settings but not in any others is not remarkable. When Jesus was teaching in the synagogue or elsewhere in a town, for example, the people listening could more easily go to and from their homes to have meals. Out in the desert, the people had nowhere to buy food. Though many Bibles and commentaries label these passages "the feeding of 4,000" or "the feeding of 5,000" or "a feeding miracle," perhaps we can gain another perspective on the stories by using a different label: "the revival in the desert."

In the passage in Mark, Jesus was preaching in the wilderness, the desert. He was far enough out of town that the crowd had stayed day and night without going home to sleep or eat. A huge crowd had followed him to this deserted area. If the people had brought provisions for a day of preaching, they had used up everything by now. Still, they had stayed. Perhaps some miraculous healings had captured their attention. Surely the preaching had been extraordinary. Why had Jesus gone into the desert to preach? If more than four thousand people had followed him to the wilderness, would twice as many have turned out to hear him if he had stayed closer to town? Maybe Jesus had not planned this huge gathering but had hoped to have some time alone with his disciples when the persistent crowd had followed. Perhaps he had moved farther and farther out of town to accommodate the growing crowd. Or perhaps preaching in the desert had been precisely his intention.

Jesus, who often withdrew to deserted places to be alone with God, understood the value of time in a harsh and sometimes threatening environment. He may have moved to the desert to preach in order to provide some aspects of this type of experience to the crowd. Although they were not experiencing the challenges and benefits of being alone, the people were removed from the comforts and distractions of home and work in this desolate place. Perhaps they stayed awake overnight because of uneasiness about what animals might be around or what unsavory characters might be passing by. They had been with Jesus for three days. Unintentionally, they had been fasting in the wilderness. In this stark environment, without adequate food or sleep, their senses might have been heightened and their resistance to hearing God's voice lessened.

Jesus acknowledged the effects of the wilderness experience on his listeners when he told his disciples that he had compassion for the crowd. He feared they might faint if they started home without eating first. After all, he had led them to the wilderness. They had fasted and listened, perhaps confronting testing and temptation within themselves. Jesus' own experience had taught him about the need to provide care for one who has been tested in the wilderness. Thus, at the end of this preaching revival, Jesus ministers to the people in another way. He feeds them until they are full and then sends them home.

Perhaps we need to listen for a call to the wilderness. Once there, we may not find much to look at—not many pictures to take with our camera. The purpose, however, is more for looking inside than outside. We need not be unsafe or miserable. The depravations we may choose are to remove distractions and sharpen our awareness of God. Jesus gave us an example of withdrawing to desert places. He invited others—his disciples and large crowds—to do the same. He invites us, too, for our souls may need the tending found only in the wilderness.

Forgiveness

Jesus taught us to ask God for forgiveness. In the Lord's Prayer as recorded in the Gospel of Luke, we read the petition to God, "Forgive us our sins" (11:4a). Jesus also taught his followers to forgive one another. When Peter asked how many times he should forgive someone for wrongs committed against him, Jesus said that Peter's suggestion of seven times was not enough. His answer was "seventy-seven times" (Matthew 18:21-22).

In what ways are we tended when we seek and offer forgiveness? In offering or in accepting forgiveness, do we tend body, heart, mind, or soul? The answer is that we may tend each one to some degree. Consider the effects of not receiving forgiveness or of withholding forgiveness from someone who has wronged you. The anger, resentment, and hurt you feel may eat at your heart, doing even further injury if the lack of forgiveness leads to a seriously damaged or broken relationship. Jesus said we are to forgive a brother and sister from our heart (Matthew 18:35b). This does not mean, however, that only the heart is tended by forgiveness. The mind may be kept from needed rest or attentive thought if wrongs are replayed over and over. The body, too, may suffer the ill effects of a troubled, angry, grieved, or guilty heart and mind. Perhaps even more than these, however, is the damage done to the soul when we do not forgive others or when we fail to seek forgiveness for ourselves. Our soul's openness to God is limited, and our relationship with God suffers until we offer forgiveness to the person who has wronged us, or accept forgiveness for ourselves.

Before looking more closely at Jesus' teaching about forgiveness, let us first consider two occasions when Jesus told individuals that their sins were forgiven. Each of the Synoptic Gospel writers recounts the story of the paralyzed man brought to Jesus by friends who avoided the crowd by lowering the man through the roof. We read in Luke, "When [Jesus] saw their faith, he said, 'Friend, your sins are forgiven you' " (5:20). The scribes and Pharisees nearby accused Jesus of blasphemy. Jesus then healed the paralyzed man so that the religious leaders would recognize his authority to forgive sins. Though Jesus acknowledged the faith of the friends, he did not comment on the faith of the paralyzed man. Nor did this man profess his faith or ask for forgiveness. Nevertheless, Jesus offered forgiveness. Perhaps in making this public announcement, Jesus freed the man from the stigma of the belief common in that day that illness and disability were due to sin. Healing the man's body alone would not have made the man whole. Forgiveness healed the rest of the man's being.

Again the Pharisees questioned Jesus' authority to forgive sins when he said that a certain woman's sins were forgiven. Upon entering the home where Jesus was eating, this woman washed his feet and anointed them with ointment (Luke 7:36-50). Jesus' host, Simon, was critical of Jesus for letting this "sinful" woman touch him. Jesus pointed out Simon's lack of hospitality and the woman's act of love. As far as we know, the woman was silent. Although she did not ask for forgiveness, her humble act of devotion and love perhaps revealed her openness to forgiveness and healing. Jesus not only told her that her sins were forgiven, but he also said to her, "Your faith has saved you; go in peace" (v. 50). In the presence of witnesses, Jesus once again affirmed someone who had been considered unclean. His words and actions declared her whole.

Let us now turn our attention to Jesus' teaching on forgiveness. Most of what we read in the Gospels suggests that forgiveness by God is conditional on our forgiveness of others. For example, following the Lord's Prayer recorded in Matthew, we read, "For if you forgive others their trespasses, your heavenly Father will also forgive you; but if you do not forgive others, neither will your Father forgive your trespasses" (6:14-15). Likewise, in Mark we read, "Whenever you stand praying, forgive, if you have anything against anyone; so that your Father in heaven may also forgive you your trespasses" (11:25). Both of these passages may be heard as "if-then" statements—if we forgive others, then God will forgive us.

Does God, in fact, withhold forgiveness until we have met certain requirements? In the two examples previously cited, Jesus offered forgiveness without any word from the recipient. He asked neither the paralyzed man nor the woman at his feet about their forgiveness of others. Consider also the parable of the Prodigal Son (Luke 15:11-32). The younger son acknowledged to himself that he had sinned against his father. The father, however, ran out to meet his son, put his arms around him, and kissed him before the son ever spoke. Though the young man confessed his sin, he did not ask for forgiveness before the father revealed his forgiveness and acceptance by calling for a grand celebration. Similarly, the father went out to the older son, not only signaling his continued love and acceptance but also directly pleading with him to join the family celebration. Although the particular sins of the older son were not specified, from his words and behavior we can identify his anger and resentment toward his father and his anger and jealousy—perhaps even hatred—toward his brother. The father's actions were an implicit offering of forgiveness without any sign of repentance or request for forgiveness by the older son. This parable suggests an unconditional love and grace, an unconditional forgiveness, from the father.

How can we reconcile these views of God's forgiveness? Perhaps the "condition" on God's forgiveness speaks more to our openness to receive it than it does to God's willingness to offer it. The prodigal son recognized his own sin and his need to ask for forgiveness from his father. He was therefore able to receive the forgiveness that already was being extended to him unconditionally. The older son was not ready, not available, to be forgiven. He did not receive forgiveness even though it was being offered to him. God's forgiveness and love are gracefully given to us. We tend our souls by forgiving others so that we may receive and experience God's forgiveness. Forgiveness of others is one important aspect of the "housecleaning of the soul" necessary to make room for knowing God, hearing God, and accepting God's forgiveness of us.

The psalmist writes, "Bless the LORD, O my soul, / and do not forget all his benefits— / who forgives all your iniquity. . . . The LORD is merciful and gracious, / slow to anger and abounding in steadfast love. . . . He does not deal with us according to our sins, / nor repay us according to our iniquities" (103:2-3a, 8, 10). Jesus' life and words about forgiveness reveal this God who offers forgiveness and love without condition. He teaches us that to experience fully God's gracious love, we must first tend our souls by forgiving others.

"Father, Forgive Them"

Two others also, who were criminals, were led away to be put to death with him. When they came to the place that is called The Skull, they crucified Jesus there with the criminals, one on his right and one on his left. Then Jesus said, "Father, forgive them; for they do not know what they are doing." And they cast lots to divide his clothing. And the people stood by, watching; but the leaders scoffed at him, saying, "He saved others; let him save himself if he is the Messiah of God, his chosen one!" The soldiers also mocked him, coming up and offering him sour wine, and saying, "If you are the King of the Jews, save yourself!" There was also an inscription over him, "This is the King of the Jews." (Luke 23:32-38)

Who heard Jesus speak these words, "Father, forgive them"? Would he have spoken these personal words to God in a voice loud enough for all those gathered around the cross to hear? Perhaps the criminals on either side heard, yet they were not around later to give a report. Many Bibles note that some ancient authorities lack verse 34, where these words are recorded. Nevertheless, the writer of these words, "Father, forgive them," thought them completely in character for Jesus to say. If the writer did not know Jesus well, he may have known others who did. At least he knew the stories about Jesus. Early followers knew that Jesus was forgiving, even to the point of forgiving those who killed him.

"Father, forgive them." Forgive whom? The Roman authorities? The Jewish religious leaders? The criminals on either side? The people who stood by watching? The disciples who had abandoned him? If Jesus wanted to forgive them all, he was offering forgiveness generously, even freely. Is the gift of forgiveness more generous than we are willing to extend to those who have wronged us? Is it more generous than we are even willing to accept for ourselves?

Jesus said, "They do not know what they are doing" (v. 34). Who did not know? The Roman authorities knew they were crucifying Jesus, the one whom Pilate refused to pronounce guilty. The Jewish religious leaders knew that they had tried to trap Jesus throughout his ministry and finally had succeeded. The criminals knew that they were guilty of their crimes. The people in the crowd knew that they had shouted to Pilate to free Barabbas and to crucify Jesus. The disciples knew that they had run away, abandoning the one they had followed, the one who had loved them for these three years. What did they *not* know? They did not know or understand fully who Jesus was. They did not understand the God that Jesus had tried to reveal to them.

We believe that Jesus was, and is, forgiving. We believe that God loves and forgives. Many times we have listened to sermons and Sunday school lessons that call us to confess and repent because of our sinful nature and our guilt. We are told that we must *ask* for forgiveness. Look, however, at the model of forgiveness in these words from the cross. Jesus asked God to forgive a group of people who did not confess their sins or repent of their sins or ask for forgiveness. He asked God to forgive people we may think do not deserve forgiveness.

Is God's forgiveness poured out to us before our confession, repentance, and humble request? If forgiveness is waiting for us, and all we must do is simply recognize and receive it, then how does God hope to elicit good behavior from us? Isn't it often the burden of guilt and the threat of punishment that keep calling us back to better behavior, back to relationship with God?

Perhaps God hopes that the gifts of our relationship with God—peace, joy, love, satisfaction, wholeness, and delight—will be enough to keep us close, as children to a parent. God sent Jesus to show us, in our own human terms, the nature of God's love for us—love given without restrictions by someone who knows us completely. God wants us to see and understand, through Jesus, the love available to us. How disappointed God must be when we talk about God's judgment and punishment as ways to push us back to God when God is offering graceful gifts to draw us close. Parents often have more success in relating to their children by offering them "carrots," or rewards, rather than "sticks," or punishments. How ironic that our Heavenly Parent offers us carrots, yet we often refuse them, insisting on sticks instead!

God freely forgives us of our sins. We must be available, however, to receive that forgiveness; and to be open and available, we must first forgive others. Forgive "her"—your mother or sister or friend or neighbor or business partner—even though she is wrong and does not deserve it. Forgive "him"—your father or brother or teacher or coach or boss—even though he is wrong and does not deserve it. Tell the person that you forgive her or him. Even if the person is dead, say, "I forgive you." The power of forgiveness is that it frees us from the life-taking burdens of anger, bitterness, resentment, and hate. When we give what is not deserved, we are free to receive what is already given to us: undeserved forgiveness from God.

"Father, forgive them." Jesus was asking God to forgive those who had wronged him—denied, betrayed, arrested, beaten, and convicted him. Why did Jesus ask for forgiveness for unnamed people who were not asking for forgiveness, who might have thought they did not need forgiveness, and who might not have heard the words spoken over them? Perhaps Jesus' words were also for the tending of his soul, the tending of his relationship with God in those difficult final hours. Jesus could not personally extend forgiveness to each person who had hurt him, but he could express his desire to forgive them—and for God to forgive them. Jesus emptied his heart and soul, letting go of every painful word and act against him. Having carefully tended his relationship with God throughout his life, he continued to tend that relationship, and his soul, by offering forgiveness. Soon he released even life itself to God: "Father, into your hands I commend my spirit" (Luke 23:46).

Prayer

As we have defined it, the soul is that part of us that hears the voice of God, experiences the presence of God, and knows God. To tend our souls, then, we must be with God and listen to God. We have considered how we may tend our souls by seeking God in the beauty of nature and in the starkness of the wilderness. For example, an ocean, mountain, garden, or forest may reveal the power, majesty, creativity, and imagination of our Creator God. Waves crashing, birds singing, and winds blowing through trees are expressions of God's voice. Likewise, we may experience and hear God in a desolate, barren place, perhaps after temporarily feeling abandoned by God. Seeking God in such places is an excellent way to tend the soul. Yet perhaps the one practice most intentionally directed toward hearing, experiencing, and knowing God—and thus tending the soul—is prayer.

Prayer can take place in the beauty of nature, in the barrenness of wilderness or desert, in a sanctuary, in a house, in a car, in an office—*anywhere*. Though prayer requires no particular outside environment, it does require a particular inside environment. To tend the soul through prayer is to quiet body, heart, mind, and soul—to be with God without distraction. Soul-tending prayer is not some obligatory, habitual "thank you God for this and that" kind of praying. Rather, it is listening more than talking, opening up every part of one's self, and being receptive to every possibility. Jesus not only taught about prayer but also modeled it, tending his own soul through prayer.

Much of what Jesus taught about prayer had to do with how and what we are *not* to pray. He saw that the religious leaders were setting a bad example in the way that they prayed, perhaps causing "ordinary" Jews to feel inadequate to the task and unworthy of taking God's time. On one occasion, he said, "Do not be like the hypocrites; for they love to stand and pray in the synagogues . . . so that they may be seen by others" (Matthew 6:5). Likewise, he warned, "Do not heap up empty phrases" (Matthew 6:7). He also cautioned against the practice of scribes who, "for the sake of appearance say long prayers" (Mark 12:38, 40). Clearly, Jesus was critical of the "showy" prayers of the religious leaders, who seemed more concerned with impressing other Jews who were listening than with directing their prayers to the most important listener, God. In the parable of the Pharisee and the Tax Collector, Jesus further denounced self-centered and self-serving prayers, warning that the Pharisee who exalted himself would be humbled (Luke 18:9-14). Such warnings are enough to give pause to anyone offering public prayers!

Jesus also gave instruction about how and what we *are* to pray. His most familiar teaching, of course, is the Lord's Prayer, which serves as a model for the content of our prayers (Matthew 6:9-13). Jesus also instructed us to pray for our enemies (Matthew 5:44), to go in a room and close the door (Matthew 6:6), to forgive others (Mark 11:25), and to pray constantly without giving up (Luke 18:1). As always, he followed his teaching in his own practice.

Though the gospel writers record several specific occasions when Jesus prayed, we may assume that Jesus prayed far more often than is recorded. No doubt he prayed regularly with and for his disciples, before serving and eating meals, and when he taught, preached, and healed. Nevertheless, we can gain insight into Jesus' soul-tending experience of prayer by looking at the specific references mentioned in the Gospels.

The Gospel of Luke gives the most extensive record of times when Jesus prayed. We read that after he had been baptized, Jesus prayed; and as he prayed, a voice from heaven proclaimed, "You are my Son, the Beloved" (3:21-22). As Jesus began his ministry—soon attracting large and growing crowds wanting to be healed and to hear him teach—we read that "he would withdraw to deserted places and pray" (5:16). In the face of mounting criticism from the Pharisees, and just prior to choosing the twelve disciples, Jesus went out alone to pray (6:12). Later in Luke we read that Jesus prayed before asking his disciples, "Who do the crowds say that I am?" (9:18). Likewise, we learn that he prayed with Peter, James, and John before the transfiguration (9:28-36); he prayed before the disciples asked him to teach them to pray (11:1); and he prayed in Gethsemane before his arrest (22:39-46).

When facing overwhelming demands and exhausting, long hours of work, Jesus prayed. When experiencing the high spiritual moments of God's presence, such as at his baptism and on the mountain when he was transfigured, Jesus prayed. When attacked by his enemies, Jesus prayed. When preparing to instruct his disciples in prayer, Jesus prayed. When making the major decision to call twelve men, he prayed. When nearing his moment of greatest challenge, pain, and need, Jesus prayed. We can only speculate about his needs in those times. Did he need the comfort, strength, and encouragement throughout his ministry that we surely would have needed under such taxing demands? Did he need to come before God with praise and thanksgiving and to humble himself when God's presence was most dramatically revealed? Did he need patience and wisdom before responding to attacks? Did he need discernment for making decisions or for choosing the right time to ask important questions?

Regardless of the various reasons for Jesus' prayers, the fact remains that Jesus chose to pray before, during, and after significant events in his life and ministry. At these times, he had particular needs that called him to prayer. The gospel writers recognized these occasions of prayer as different from all the others. Jesus wanted to hear the voice of God, to feel the presence of God with him, and to know God and God's will. To hear, feel, and know another person in a relationship, we must spend intentional and attentive time with that person. Jesus spent this kind of time with God. He tended his soul with prayer.

"There He Prayed"

In the morning, while it was still very dark, he got up and went out to a deserted place, and there he prayed. (Mark 1:35)
Now during those days he went out to the mountain to pray; and he spent the night in prayer to God. (Luke 6:12)

Jesus prayed at all the usual, expected times. We know, for example, that he blessed the bread before breaking and passing it. Because he practiced what he preached and taught, we may assume he did not stand in the synagogue praying loudly for all to hear. Rather, he withdrew to quiet places to pray. Perhaps he would go to a quiet room in the house where he was staying or find a spot outside under a tree. These two passages reveal that Jesus did not limit himself to a daily "quiet time" of Scripture reading and prayer. He got up in the dark of early morning and went out alone to pray. Another time he went out alone and prayed through an entire night. Nothing we read here or elsewhere in the Gospels suggests that Jesus was challenging and testing himself during these extended times of prayer. He did not have to force himself to get up at four o'clock in the morning to pray, and he did not have to "watch the clock" in order to stay awake a whole night in prayer. For Jesus, praying was not like a new exercise or diet plan designed to cause maximum sacrifice and to test endurance. He needed and wanted to pray. In fact, the Scriptures seem to suggest that he was *eager* to pray, for he had much to process in his mind and his heart—as well as stress to release from his body and mind. Jesus centered himself and tended his soul by spending extended time with God in prayer.

According to the account in Mark, Jesus had been teaching in the synagogue in Capernaum before he went to Simon's house and healed

Simon's mother-in-law of a fever. That same evening at sundown, people from town started bringing sick or demon-possessed friends and family to him to be healed. We read that, "The whole city was gathered around the door" (1:33). Given the size of the crowd, we might speculate that this healing session went late into the night. We know from other gospel accounts that Jesus could feel the power leaving him when he healed someone, suggesting it was a physical experience. Hour after hour, person after person, with family members crowding in and demons shouting, Jesus healed. At what hour did Jesus stop and try to go to bed? Could he possibly go to sleep after such an intense evening?

The very next morning, "while it was still very dark, he got up and went out to a deserted place, and there he prayed" (v. 35). Perhaps he had not slept at all. The previous day and night had been unsettling, and Jesus needed time alone with God. Yet why did he go to a deserted place? Capernaum is by the Sea of Galilee. Why choose the barren desert over the calming waters? Of course, we cannot know. Perhaps he returned to an environment similar to his place of testing where he had found wisdom, strength, and direction. Perhaps the previous twenty-four hours had felt like another time of testing.

Continuing with the account in Mark, we learn that while Jesus was out, probably after morning light, Simon and the others back at the house missed him. "Simon and his companions hunted for him. When they found him, they said to him, 'Everyone is searching for you'" (1:36-37). Did Jesus return to the house to eat? When did he get any rest? Later, Jesus' family was concerned that he had lost his mind (3:19b-35). No doubt the reports of demons shouting at him and his shouting back, as well as his open defiance of the religious leaders, contributed to their concern. Perhaps his brothers also had talked with some of the disciples who had told them stories about Jesus' late nights and early mornings and long hours spent who-knows-where. Of course, Jesus did not always keep such hours. He tended his body with food and rest. Still, sometimes the tending of one aspect of our being must be compromised to tend another. When we are sick, for example, we may appropriately neglect the relationships our hearts need or the mental exercise our minds need. Likewise, when we are drained and unsettled spiritually, our soul tending may require that our bodies get by on a little less sleep.

More than once in his ministry, Jesus needed to tend his soul in ways that may have compromised temporarily the tending of his body. The writer of the Gospel of Luke reports, "Now during those days . . . " During those days of preaching, healing, teaching, and arguing with the Pharisees about Sabbath laws, Jesus spent an entire night in prayer (Luke 6:12). This time Jesus chose a mountain setting for extended prayer—perhaps because it offered him a place for some time alone. What's more, the mountain was still relatively close to the large group of disciples who were waiting for him. Following this night of prayer, Jesus called from among this group twelve men "whom he also named apostles" (6:13). The text suggests that this long night of prayer was at least in part for the purpose of discerning whom he would call. As the twelve disciples came down the mountain with Jesus, they were met by a "great multitude" of people gathered down below, many of them wanting to be healed. We read that "all in the crowd were trying to touch him, for power came out from him and healed all of them" (6:19). Though he was certainly exhausted after this experience, from both the lack of sleep and the physical demands of healing, he had tended his soul well. He had chosen twelve men to help him in his ministry and to help him tend his heart.

In the early morning and through the night, Jesus prayed alone. Although these extended times of prayer recorded in the Gospels were related to major events and decisions in his life, this does not mean that Jesus sometimes needed God more than other times. No, Jesus always needed and always tended his relationship with God. Still, some of his experiences required him to compromise body, heart, and mind in order to focus all his attention on soul listening and being with God. Certain challenges called for more time in prayer. For Jesus, prayer was the source of strength, comfort, wisdom, and reassurance for his soul. We might say that prayer was his soul's delight.

Obedience

The rich young ruler told Jesus that he had obeyed all the commandments. Jesus knew, however, that the young man was separated from God, and that following God with his whole heart, soul, mind, and strength required one more thing: selling all his possessions. The young man was not expecting this request. He had been confident that he was in good standing with God and that Jesus would praise his obedience to the law. Yet Jesus clearly indicated that being obedient to God meant more than following any law or rule or standard.

Obedience does not look the same for everyone. Being obedient to God means following the path of God's call to each one of us. It means following God's leadership in every aspect of our lives. Our souls discern whom God has created and called us to be. To find the path of God's will for our lives and keep walking along it, we must listen and question—and listen carefully again. Then, like Jesus, we tend our souls by staying on the path.

How did Jesus discern his path of obedience? And was walking the path an easy task for him?

According to the gospel accounts, Jesus' first act of obedience as an adult was to be baptized by John the Baptist. The voice from heaven proclaimed, "You are my Son, the Beloved; with you I am well pleased" (Luke 3:22b). If only we received such unmistakable affirmation of our decisions as Jesus received for his! Following his baptism, Jesus spent forty days in the wilderness. Perhaps his time there was a significant part of his soul-searching to know who he was and to discern the path God was calling him to follow. That his soul had heard the voice of God in answer to his searching is evident in his responses to the challenges posed to him by Satan. Jesus met each temptation with a reply from Scripture, indicating that his authority and power were from God and were not to be misused or traded for selfish gain.

During his ministry, Jesus was challenged in another way. In the Gospel of John we read that Jesus crossed the Sea of Galilee, and "a large crowd kept following him" (6:1-2). Though Jesus and his disciples went up a mountain, the crowd began to come toward him. Recognizing their need, Jesus fed about five thousand people a meal of bread and fish. The people were amazed by this act. Then we read these words: "When Jesus realized that they were about to come and take him by force to make him king, he withdrew again to the mountain by himself" (v. 15). Jesus withdrew to the mountain for more soul-searching time with God. We cannot know what Jesus was thinking or feeling or what he was praying during this time alone. Perhaps he needed to reaffirm his understanding of who God was calling him to be.

Certainly, he continued to tend his soul—particularly through prayer—in order to stay true to God's call.

The Gospel of John indicates that Jesus often clearly stated his obedience to God's will. For example, when the disciples were trying to get Jesus to eat, he responded, "My food is to do the will of him who sent me and to complete his work" (4:34). Similarly, Jesus was teaching in Jerusalem when he said, "I can do nothing on my own. As I hear, I judge; and my judgment is just, because I seek to do not my own will but the will of him who sent me" (5:30). Later, while teaching in Capernaum, Jesus said, "I have come down from heaven, not to do my own will, but the will of him who sent me" (6:38). Without a doubt, Jesus was totally committed to doing God's will and following the path in keeping with that will. Yet the Scriptures suggest that even Jesus may have had questions about that path at times.

Later in the Gospel of John, we read of Jesus' struggle in his soul. After being welcomed by a crowd carrying palm branches and shouting hosannas, Jesus said, "Now my soul is troubled. And what should I say—'Father, save me from this hour'? No, it is for this reason that I have come to this hour. Father, glorify your name" (12:27-28a). Although Jesus affirmed his intent to follow God's will as he understood it, he revealed that there was a conflict and struggle going on in his soul.

Jesus warned his disciples that following him—being obedient to the call they had heard—would be very difficult. He told them they would face persecution, betrayal, and hatred. Yet he told them, "By your endurance you will gain your souls" (Luke 21:19). As the most difficult time of testing drew near for the disciples, Peter underestimated how hard obedience would be. When Jesus told the disciples, "You will all become deserters because of me this night," Peter claimed he would never leave Jesus. Then, when Jesus said that Peter would, in fact, deny him, Peter said he would die with Jesus before he would deny him (Matthew 26:31-35). As we learn from Peter, knowing God's will may not be easy, but being obedient to what we do know of God's will may be far more difficult. That, however, is the work of tending the soul: to know and to follow.

To stay on the path of God's calling, we must tend our own souls. Jesus shows us how to tend our souls by spending time in the beauty and the starkness of nature. He also teaches us to tend our souls by offering forgiveness and praying. The ultimate purpose of tending our souls in all of these ways is to discern God's will and to gain strength for the journey along that path. The soul rests in its relationship with God through a continuing pilgrimage of obedience to God's calling. Yet the question persists: If Jesus struggled in his soul to remain obedient, how can we hope to endure? Perhaps we can find some strength, comfort, and hope in Jesus' words to us: "Come to me, all you that are weary and are carrying heavy burdens, and I will give you rest. Take my yoke upon you, and learn from me; for I am gentle and humble in heart, and you will find rest for your souls" (Matthew 11:28-29).

"Not What I Want"

Then Jesus went with them to a place called Gethsemane; and he said to his disciples, "Sit here while I go over there and pray." He took with him Peter and the two sons of Zebedee, and began to be grieved and agitated. Then he said to them, "I am deeply grieved, even to death; remain here, and stay awake with me." And going a little farther, he threw himself on the ground and prayed, "My Father, if it is possible, let this cup pass from me; yet not what I want but what you want." Then he came to the disciples and found them sleeping; and he said to Peter, "So, could you not stay awake with me one hour? Stay awake and pray that you may not come into the time of trial; the spirit indeed is willing, but the flesh is weak." Again he went away for the second time and prayed, "My Father, if this cannot pass unless I drink it, your will be done." Again he came and found them sleeping, for their eyes were heavy. So leaving them again, he went away and prayed for the third time, saying the same words. Then he came to the disciples and said to them, "Are you still sleeping and taking your rest? See, the hour is at hand, and the Son of Man is betrayed into the hands of sinners. Get up, let us be going. See, my betrayer is at hand." (Matthew 26:36-46)

The Apostle Paul wrote that Jesus "became obedient to the point of death— / even death on a cross" (Philippians 2:8). We are told that as he prayed in the garden, Jesus repeated these words to God three times: "Your will be done" (Matthew 26:42). Clearly Jesus desired to be obedient to God. Although he relinquished his will to God, Jesus' prayer in the garden also revealed an inner struggle to follow the path he saw before him. Jesus asked, or possibly even pleaded, "Let this cup pass from me." Then he added, "Yet not what I want but what you want" (v. 39). His spirit was willing, but, at least for a moment, his flesh was weak. Perhaps just moments later, he made this very remark to his sleepy disciples: "The spirit indeed is willing, but the flesh is weak" (v. 41).

Was facing the physical pain, the agony of death by crucifixion, the only aspect of this "cup" that Jesus did not want to swallow? Such a conclusion misses other aspects of the agony of these final moments before his arrest. We know that Jesus expected one of his disciples to betray him and the other eleven to desert him. He had shared his life and ministry with these men; he had sent them out as missionaries to preach good news and heal the sick. Could he have wondered what would become of them now—and of the work he had begun with them? Is it possible that he might have questioned whether anyone would remember who, and in whose name, this work had been done? Jesus had challenged the religious leaders, attacking their interpretation of the law and attempting to show them a different image of God. These same leaders had plotted to kill him. Did Jesus possibly think he had failed? In the midst of this intense struggle in body, heart, mind, and soul, how did Jesus remain faithful and obedient to God's call? He prepared himself, tending his whole being in every possible way—right up to the moment at which Judas arrived to betray him.

Jesus did not ever give up on what he had been called to be and to do. Recognizing the approaching end, he did not stop his work, internally or externally, and wait to be arrested. In fact, in the final week before his death, Jesus continued tending his body, heart, mind, and soul as he had done throughout his ministry.

How did Jesus tend his body during the week in Jerusalem, which began with a full day of celebration, arguments, and healings? The Gospels suggest that he ate healthy food, exercised, rested, and was touched in healing ways. The first evening of the week, rather than stay overnight in Jerusalem, he wisely went out to Bethany where he might have a better chance to rest his body (Matthew 21:17). There Jesus and the disciples were probably fed and cared for by the women who, as we learn later, had come to Jerusalem with him (Matthew 27:55). One evening later in the week, after walking out to Bethany once more, he went to the house of Simon the leper where a woman anointed his head with ointment (Matthew 26:6-7). Surely the brief walks to Bethany, the hospitality of food and lodging, and the anointing—and perhaps physical embraces—all tended his body well.

Jesus also exercised and rested his mind regularly throughout the week in Jerusalem. He exercised his mind by teaching, debating, and telling parables as he had always done. Likewise, he exercised his sharp wit when he told the Pharisees that the stones would shout in praise of him even if the crowd were quiet (Luke 19:40), and when he answered the Pharisees' question about paying taxes to the emperor (Matthew 22:15-22). He also rested his mind by confronting his enemies in Jerusalem during the day and getting away from controversy in the evenings in Bethany. Similarly, by allowing his disciples and other friends to handle the details of lodging and meals, including the Passover meal, he limited possible mental distractions and stresses.

Jesus tended the emotions of his heart during the week in Jerusalem as well. For example, he unleashed his anger against the money changers in the temple, and preached passionately, and with anger, against the Pharisees and scribes (Matthew 21:12; 23:1-36). Even as cruel treatment awaited him, Jesus continued to show compassion—curing the blind and lame in the temple, staying in the home of a leper, and defending the woman who anointed him with oil. Jesus also nurtured his closest relationships throughout the week. He withdrew to the Mount of Olives for private time with his disciples (Matthew 24:3). Later, he gathered with his disciples for a final time of fellowship around the table, sharing the Passover meal with them. The occasion was a time of honesty, intimacy, and passion. Jesus tended his heart well during this week filled with deep emotion.

Finally, during these last days of his ministry, Jesus carefully tended his soul. After the Passover meal, Jesus took his disciples with him to Gethsemane. He intentionally went to a quiet and familiar place, a garden where he could tend his soul. There he asked Peter, James, and John—the three with whom he was closest—to go a little farther with him to pray. Having tended body, heart, mind, and soul throughout this most difficult week, Jesus now focused on his troubled soul by praying.

He asked his best friends to be a supportive presence and to pray with him, telling them of the deep struggle of his soul: "I am deeply grieved, even to death" (26:38). Having prepared himself for this moment as well as he could, Jesus still needed these three friends to be with him. He needed to be with God and to know and feel God's presence with him.

As noted previously, Jesus searched his soul and asked God to "let this cup pass from me" (v. 39). In other words, "Can you find another path for me? Is there some other way, God, to accomplish what we want to do?" Jesus was completely honest with himself and with God. Although three times he asked God to show him a different path, each time Jesus clearly relinquished his own desire to God's desire. His final affirmation to himself and to God was that God's will be done. His understanding of God's reply, that the cup would not be taken away, was revealed as he immediately gathered his disciples and went to face his betrayer. After his soulful struggle, Jesus not only had assurance about the path he should follow but also had the courage and the strength to keep following that path to the end, even though it would not be easy. During this most difficult week on this most difficult path, Jesus was obedient to God. When he finished praying, he looked up and saw that Judas was approaching. To his disciples he said, "Get up, let us be going" (v. 46). He knew he needed to trust God and to keep walking.

How can we hope to be obedient when we must struggle, even to the point of death? We can follow Jesus' example by continuing to tend body, heart, mind, and soul. We can be honest in our struggle—with ourselves, with our closest family and friends, and with God. We can pray without ceasing. Then, we can look up and keep walking. When we arrive at such a point in our lives, we may hear Jesus' words spoken to his disciples as words spoken personally to us: "Let us be going." Jesus offers us comfort and strength, his very presence with us, as we walk our own paths in obedience to God.

Questions for Reflection and Discussion

1. How does your soul hear the voice of God or experience the presence of God?

2. Reflect on the condition of your soul. Is it "lost"? Alert? Quiet? Troubled? Prayerfully consider the kind of tending your soul needs right now.

3. Visualize your favorite place of natural beauty, perhaps a vacation spot. What about this place touches you or makes you smile with delight or helps you feel close to God? How often do you spend time in this place—or other places of natural beauty? How are these times part of following Jesus?

4. Perhaps the place you named in question 3 is far from where you live. Find a closer spot—a park or garden or field or porch or even a window view. Jesus told a parable saying, "Look at the fig tree and all the trees; as soon as they sprout leaves you can see for yourselves and know that summer is already near" (Luke 21:29-30). Practice looking for signs, evidence of the Creator God, using the "look, see, and know" process suggested by the parable. What do you observe by looking and seeing that helps you to know that God is near? How can this "look, see, and know" process help you develop a more intentional daily connection to God?

5. What do you think and how do you feel about the possibility that Jesus might have been tempted during his ministry to give up or to exploit his power? Whether he was tempted or not, we know that he stayed true to his calling. How does knowing this encourage you? What help can you find in Jesus' example for your own temptations?

6. Why do you think we rarely hear and follow the call to embrace the wilderness as a spiritual experience? Can you give some modern examples of those who experience God in the solitude of the wilderness? Jesus clearly valued and learned from his wilderness experience. What can we learn from Jesus and others about the value of wilderness? Have you ever been invited to such an experience? If so, what was the result? If not, what might prevent you from hearing or answering such a call?

7. "For if you forgive others their trespasses, your heavenly father will also forgive you" (Matthew 6:14). Is God's forgiveness of us conditional? Does God withhold forgiveness based on the quality or sincerity of our forgiveness of others? In what ways does being forgiven and forgiving others tend body, heart, mind, and soul?

8. Jesus criticized prayers for show and taught us to go into a room and close the door when we pray. What, then, is the purpose of public prayer? What is the value of public prayer? What are the dangers of public prayer?

9. What occasions in your life have caused you to spend more time in prayer than usual? Why did you choose to pray more during those times? Look again at the occasions noted in the Gospels when Jesus prayed. What similarities do you find in Jesus' experience and your own?

10. Jesus wanted and needed to spend extended time with God. His prayer habits probably reflect desire more than duty. Do you ever experience prayer as your "soul's delight"? Describe the circumstances when you have felt most eager, or least eager, to pray, and those when prayer was most or least meaningful to you. How can you maintain or recover prayer that tends the soul?

11. We talk of searching for God's will, but perhaps we need to look long and hard at what we already know about God's will. Think about the way Jesus lived—who he was and what he did. Think about his preaching and teaching. Then make a list of what you know to be God's will for disciples of Jesus. What does our constant questioning about knowing God's will reveal about our willingness to obey what we *do* know about God's call to us?

12. Do you think that obedience to authority figures—parents, teachers, law enforcement officials, those in charge in businesses or government—is declining or increasing in our society? What evidence do you see for your answer? Do you think there is a connection between the degree of our obedience to authority in society and our obedience to God? Why or why not? Do you think we can be on our path of obedience to God while being disobedient to authorities we face? Why or why not? What guidance can you find in the Gospels or elsewhere in Scripture that relates directly to the issue of obedience to earthly authorities and to God?

5. Tending Toward Wholeness: Interconnections

WE HAVE LOOKED AT EACH ASPECT OF OUR BEING—BODY, HEART, MIND, and soul—as if we were the sum of disconnected parts. No one part, however, functions independently of the others. While a certain activity may be intended to tend one particular aspect of who we are, most often it also will nurture other aspects of our being to some degree. Similarly, neglecting one part of our being generally causes problems for other parts of our total self.

When writing to the church at Corinth, Paul used specific parts of the physical body as an analogy to talk about the body of Christ, the church, and the value of all members and their various gifts: "As it is, there are many members, yet one body. The eye cannot say to the hand, 'I have no need of you,' nor again the head to the feet, 'I have no need of you'" (1 Corinthians 12:20-21). We might rewrite Paul's words as follows: "The body cannot say to the heart, 'I have no need of you,' nor the mind to the soul, 'I have no need of you.'" All aspects of our being are essential. All are created to function together.

Consider this example of the interconnectedness of body, heart, mind, and soul. Rest, such as sitting down in a chair to relax or going to bed for sufficient hours of sleep, is necessary to tend the body. What happens to us if we do not rest? Our bodies feel tired and our eyes become heavy. We may lack the energy to make it through the day. Yet does only the body suffer? Of course not. The mind is fueled by adequate sleep, too. Without it, we cannot stay alert, think clearly, or reason carefully. Similarly, the heart and soul bear a burden when we do not get adequate rest. We cannot control our emotions as well when we are exhausted. For example, we may unleash our anger in inappropriate ways or cry tears of grief long after the worst of the pain has been resolved. Without adequate rest, we surely will not have the strength to withstand the wilderness. We may not even have the strength to spend fifteen minutes in prayer. Rest tends the whole being.

Consider another example. We have said that relationships tend the heart. Good friends help us process the strong emotions of our hearts, such as providing care and concern during times of grief or helping us find opportunities for expressing our passion. Likewise, families provide companionship, nurture, support, and more. Yet, relationships tend more than the heart. A vigorous friend may volunteer to be our partner for regular exercise, or a spouse, intimate friend, or child may offer a comforting embrace. In both cases, the relationships tend the body as well as the heart. By helping us laugh at our mistakes and challenging us to think creatively and analytically, a coworker may help us tend our minds and hearts. A close companion may help us tend our soul by teaching us about forgiveness or making us pause to watch a heron take off in flight across a marsh. A friend may offer to pray for us and ask us to pray for her as well. Relationships tend not only the heart, but also the body, mind, and soul.

Certainly in Jesus we see more than the sum of isolated parts. From a very young age, he was on a pilgrimage toward wholeness. After he was dedicated in the temple and the family returned to Nazareth, we read: "The child grew and became strong, filled with wisdom; and the favor of God was upon him" (Luke 2:40). Later, twelve-year-old Jesus was found talking with religious leaders in the temple. The gospel writer tells us that after his parents took him home, "Jesus increased in wisdom and in years, and in divine and human favor" (Luke 2:52). Jesus grew up, becoming older and taller and stronger. He grew not only in wisdom but also in favor with other people and with God. These words suggest a healthy tending of body, heart, mind, and soul. In his early years, Jesus benefited from the nurture of his parents and other adults. The story of the boy Jesus in the temple indicates self-awareness and understanding at a young age. These brief accounts in the Gospel of Luke suggest that, from his youth, in the ways we have identified and more, Jesus tended himself toward wholeness.

Many times throughout this book, when we have discussed how Jesus pursued an activity that tended one aspect of his being, we have noted that other aspects also were tended. For example, Jesus tended his body by walking. Certainly it was wonderful exercise that strengthened his physical heart, lowered his cholesterol, helped control his weight, and benefited his body in so many other ways. While getting this exercise, however, he often tended heart, mind, and soul as well.

In the Gospel of Matthew we read of one walking expedition early in Jesus' ministry: "As he walked by the Sea of Galilee, [Jesus] saw two brothers, Simon, who is called Peter, and Andrew his brother, casting a net into the sea—for they were fishermen. And he said to them, 'Follow me, and I will make you fish for people.' Immediately they left their nets and followed him" (4:18-20). Jesus was walking by the sea, exercising his body. Perhaps he had gone there to draw closer to God as he enjoyed the sights and sounds of the sea. He might have been praying for discernment in choosing his disciples, the men who would help him in his ministry. Jesus looked out and saw fishermen. Perhaps he paused to reflect on these two men in particular. He might have known of them and their family. Should he be open to recruiting fishermen rather than religious men who were trained more thoroughly in the law and in practices of the faith? Jesus saw in Peter and Andrew qualities that he needed. He knew how to approach them and what kind of heartfelt response he desired to see in them. "Follow me," he said, and the two men joined him on his journey. Clearly this walk tended Jesus' soul, mind, and heart as well as his body.

On another occasion, Jesus took advantage of an opportunity to teach the disciples as they were walking along together (Mark 9:30-37). He began to unburden his heart by telling them of his betrayal and death. At one point, he walked ahead of the others. Perhaps he was thinking about next steps in his ministry, or new examples for parables, or responses to the Pharisees' questions and criticisms. Perhaps he was praying. We cannot know what he was thinking or doing as he walked along, but we do know that he overheard the disciples arguing about who was the greatest. They probably expressed some honest ambition and even some anger as they walked and argued. Later, after arriving at a house in Capernaum, Jesus questioned his disciples about their argument. He tried to teach them a crucial lesson about his kingdom, saying, "Whoever wants to be first must be last of all and servant of all" (Mark 9:35). No doubt Jesus knew that walking sometimes helps with talking—about ideas and decisions in the mind as well as about aches and issues of the heart.

Another activity that often nurtured Jesus' body, heart, mind, and soul was a shared meal. After being called from his tax collector's booth to be a follower of Jesus, Levi gave a banquet in Jesus' honor (Luke 5:29-39). On this and similar occasions, the meal was about more than tending the body with food and rest. In calling Levi to be a disciple and agreeing to dine with tax collectors and sinners, Jesus was expressing his passion for the inclusion of these and other "outcasts" in the king-dom of God. He opened his own heart to these people in spite of harsh criticism from the religious leaders. On this occasion, Jesus had to be mentally quick to respond to the Pharisees' attacks about the company he was keeping and the eating and drinking habits he and his disciples were practicing. No doubt this meal included a lively exchange of views. Although the description of the banquet at Levi's house does not explicitly record the soul-tending experience of blessing or giving thanks for the bread, other shared meals, including all the accounts of the feedings of thousands, do so.

Walking, sharing meals, and many other activities we have dis-cussed tended all aspects of Jesus' being—body, heart, mind, and soul. Yet another essential ingredient evident in Jesus' tending toward wholeness was balance among all his tending activities and among each aspect of his being. For example, Jesus often argued at length with the Pharisees, but sometimes he walked away—protecting his mind and body from exhaustion and his heart from uncontrolled anger. Jesus pursued his passion for justice and showed compassion for the poor, but sometimes he left the crowd waiting and wanting more—avoiding burnout in his body and spirit. Sometimes he called for selling everything and giving it all to the poor, but once he affirmed Mary and her extravagant gesture of pouring costly perfume on his feet. Balance for Jesus was not a life of cautious moderation in all things. It was closer to a life of balancing extremes—days of preaching and healing followed by private retreat; hours of heated debate followed by quiet prayer alone; vigorous, long hours of walking followed by complete rest.

Following Jesus' example means that we cannot pursue one activity while ignoring the others. Exercise without rest does not tend body or mind. Tending anger while ignoring grief will not help the heart. Spending time in the wilderness without forgiving others will not heal the soul. Balance within and among all the parts is essential.

Jesus knew from Hebrew Scripture that God is interested in the whole person. When asked which commandment is the greatest, Jesus replied, "You shall love the Lord your God with all your heart, and with all your soul, and with all your mind, and with all your strength" (Mark 12:30). Loving God is more than an activity of the heart. It is more than a response from the soul. It requires more than belief in the mind. It entails more than using the strength of the body in service to God. The law suggests that every part of our being must join together in loving God: "You shall love the Lord your God with all your heart, and with all your soul, and with all your mind, and with all your strength" (Mark 12:30). Jesus added a second commandment: "You shall love your neighbor as yourself" (Mark 12:31). As he taught and exemplified in his own living, Jesus showed us that God desires us to love God and others with our whole being. Loving God and neighbor as the laws demand calls us to be whole by following Jesus in tending our own body, heart, mind, and soul.

What does it mean for us to be whole? Acknowledging that Jesus is whole is an easy first step, but understanding and applying his example to our own lives may leave us puzzled. Is wholeness something we must achieve before we can love God? To answer this question, let us consider the meaning of the word. *Whole* means "complete." If someone eats a whole pie, for example, we know that this person ate all of it, without leaving any pieces. Similarly, we may think of wholeness in a person as meaning healthy in all the parts—body, heart, mind, and soul. These definitions, however, may not be adequate or appropriate to describe the wholeness that God desires for each of us.

What about the person who is blind and the person who has had a disfiguring accident or surgery? Can these persons be whole in their bodies? What of the woman who has deep emotional scars from abuse or neglect, or the man who has been rejected or disowned by his family? Can these persons be whole in their hearts? Is wholeness of mind possible for one who has mental illness or serious learning disabilities?

Is wholeness of soul possible for someone who has been told only of a wrathful God, or one who has been hurt by church leaders "in the name of God"? Can any of these persons be whole?

Tending toward wholeness does not require having the body of a marathon runner or the mind of a brilliant teacher. It does not mean that persons with wounds or scars in their hearts and souls are ineligible. Wholeness is not an achievement or goal met by going down a "tending" checklist: exercise program, strict diet, eight hours of sleep, anger management classes, grief recovery support group, crossword puzzles, regular trips to the ocean, disciplined prayer routine, and on and on. No one could be whole if the requirements were to *be* perfect or to *do* our tending perfectly.

Wholeness is how God made us, how God sees us, and how God's own image lies within us. Wholeness in relationship to God and others is God's desire for each one of us. It involves first seeing ourselves as children of God made in the image of God, and then trying to live in that vision. Tending toward wholeness is a pilgrimage with God that accepts our starting points, our limitations, and our woundedness in body, heart, mind, and soul.

Wholeness is finding our completion in being the persons God has created us to be. It will look different in each of us and *be* different for each of us. Our standard is never the example of another person. Such comparisons are unhelpful and miss the point. What is important is how each of us is tending our own body, heart, mind, and soul. A critical question to ask is this: *Am I moving along my own path on my own pilgrimage, and am I focusing on being the person God is calling me to be?*

Jesus is our model for tending ourselves toward wholeness. Looking at Jesus helps us learn how to care for ourselves—body, heart, mind, and soul. His healing ministry was directed toward the whole person. He healed broken bodies and broken minds. He healed wounded hearts and wounded souls. Following Jesus also means tending others. Though God calls us to our own particular path toward wholeness, a daily path that extends until death, God also calls us to help others begin and continue their own pilgrimages.

My tending will not look like your tending. My process of becoming whole will not look like yours. We will remain as different as Peter was from John, and as different as Mary was from Martha. We all, however, share one thing in common: We are all listening to and accepting the call we hear from Jesus, who says, "Come, follow me."

"I Have Eagerly Desired to Eat . . . with You"

When the hour came, he took his place at the table, and the apostles with him. He said to them, "I have eagerly desired to eat this Passover with you before I suffer; for I tell you, I will not eat it until it is fulfilled in the kingdom of God." Then he took a cup, and after giving thanks he said, "Take this and divide it among yourselves; for I tell you that from now on I will not drink of the fruit of the vine until the kingdom of God comes." Then he took a loaf of bread, and when he had given thanks, he broke it and gave it to them, saying, "This is my body, which is given for you. Do this in remembrance of me." And he did the same with the cup after supper, saying, "This cup that is poured out for you is the new covenant in my blood." (Luke 22:14-20)

Jesus and his disciples were gathered around a table. The occasion was one of religious significance—they were celebrating Passover by eating the traditional Passover meal. These thirteen men were sharing a special time of fellowship. The disciples did not yet know how significant this particular meal would be for them. They did not know this meal was the last one that all of them would have together.

From the descriptions of this evening recorded in the Gospels, we can see many ways in which the body, heart, mind, and soul of each man may have been tended. First, how were the bodies of these men tended? Perhaps when Jesus arrived for the meal, he embraced each man. We can imagine that the growing agony in his heart and the overflowing compassion for each man, even for Judas—perhaps especially for Judas—would cause Jesus to want to hold each one before sitting down to the meal. We know that they were resting, reclining next to one another around the table. We also know that the food of this special meal, though not their usual diet, would tend the body well.

How were their hearts tended on this occasion? Of course, the existing relationships among these men had tended the hearts of each one prior to this evening. Yet surely their hearts were tended this night as they talked and ate. Though we do not know all they said to one another, Mark's account records this comment of Jesus: "Truly I tell you, one of you will betray me, one who is eating with me" (Mark 14:18). As he had done throughout their time together, Jesus talked about the grief and pain in his heart. The disciples immediately experienced their own distress. They, too, had learned to express their mental and heartfelt concerns. One and then another asked Jesus, "Surely, not I?" (Mark 14:19).

Jesus' mind was likely in a state of heightened awareness and attentiveness on this night. He greeted them by saying, "I have eagerly desired to eat this Passover with you before I suffer, for I tell you, I will not eat it until it is fulfilled in the kingdom of God" (Luke 22:15). Clearly he had anticipated the occasion and had thought about the significance of this meal with these companions, as well as what awaited him. Surely the conversation among the men exercised Jesus' mind. Furthermore, his words later in the evening indicated profound thought and reflection: "This is my body, which is given for you. . . . This cup that is poured out for you is the new covenant in my blood" (Luke 22:19-20).

What do we find in this gathering around the table that tended their souls? At the very least, we see Jesus offering prayers as he gave thanks, first for the cup and then for the bread. We also recognize Jesus' obedience to keep following God on the path to which he had been called. If we close our eyes and think about putting ourselves with these men around the table and later in the garden, our own hearts and souls may be overwhelmed with emotion. We can only imagine the depth of intensity, intimacy, and passion experienced by Jesus and the twelve on this night.

This gathering, this special meal, tended those present in yet another way. The activity of remembering, of calling forth old memories and creating new ones, tended their bodies, hearts, minds, and souls. At this meal, the sight, smell, touch, and taste of the particular foods not only tended their bodies but also their souls, helping them recall memories of previous Passover experiences. As they participated in the meal, Jesus and the disciples remembered and celebrated God's deliverance of the Israelites out of slavery in Egypt. Those around the table remembered their heritage of faith, their tradition as children of God. Practicing their faith in this way, remembering, drew these men closer to God—just as our souls are tended when we remember our heritage through symbols and celebrations. As the disciples watched Jesus bless, break, and share the bread, they remembered other meals they had shared with him. The repetition of these acts—blessing, breaking, sharing—had made them familiar. From this common experience at their last meal, Jesus created a new memory for his disciples. He shared the bread, saying it was his body. He passed the cup, saying it was his blood. Jesus touched his disciples' hearts as he asked them to think of him when, gathering again as they did that night, they "do this."

Jesus said, "Do this." What is *this* to which he referred? Is it following traditional ceremonies on special religious days? Is it gathering around the table with friends for a time of fellowship? Is it blessing, breaking, and sharing the bread? Is it eating bread and drinking wine in a special way after special words are spoken? Which of these things did Jesus want them, and us, to do? Perhaps he meant for us to do all of this. Gather around the table with friends. Talk about the thoughts of our minds and the emotions of our hearts. Listen as others do the same. Enjoy a meal together. Bless, break, and share the bread of communion. Share the cup of wine. Celebrate your heritage of faith. Perhaps in doing all of these things, we will find in this last supper a model for tending body, heart, mind, and soul. Following this example can help us walk along the path toward wholeness—being the persons God has created and called us to be.

Again, Jesus says, "Do this." Do *all* of this. And, as you do, listen for the quiet words of Jesus, "Remember me."

Questions for Reflection and Discussion

1. In what ways are body, heart, mind, and soul interconnected? Why is balance among these various aspects of our being important?

2. Consider events that can affect your whole being. For example, worrying about the choices made by a close family member may disturb your mind, upset your stomach, break your heart, and cause troubling questions in your soul. Or, perhaps a brisk, early morning walk in the park can relax your body, refresh your

mind, ease a burden in your heart, and connect your soulful self to the presence of God. Think of a personal experience that affected your whole being and made the interconnection of body, heart, mind, and soul obvious to you; or imagine or plan an experience that could tend all aspects of your being. How did your experience—or how would your imagined experience— affect your whole being? How did (or would) it specifically affect body, heart, mind, and soul?

3. Think about the concept of balance in your life in two different ways:

   a) *Within* each specific part—body, heart, mind, and soul: Do you experience a lack of balance in any area? For example, do you spend so much time showing compassion for people in need that you have too little time for close relationships that could tend your own heart? Do you "rest" your mind by passively watching television and dozing with little mental stimulation or challenge? How might you find better balance *within* each specific part of your being?

   b) *Among* the four parts functioning together as a whole: Do you experience a lack of balance in your total being? For example, do you speak and act out of your heart with little thought from your mind? Or, do you see yourself in the Pharisees, who thought they knew the law but had no compassion? Perhaps you have an active devotional life but neglect care of your body. How might you bring balance *among* all four dimensions of your being?

4. What does it mean to love God with your body (your strength)? With your mind? With your heart? With your soul? Give specific examples.

5. Jesus showed us not only how to live, but also how to die. Take time to read at least one gospel account of the last week of Jesus' life. Make a list of every aspect of tending body, heart, mind, or soul that you observe. (The scripture reflection "I Have Eagerly Desired to Eat . . . with You" highlighted some of these. Note these as you read while looking for others.) What insights does Jesus' example offer of how we can best tend ourselves as we prepare for the end of life—or as we tend a loved one who is

dying? (Note: Because Jesus was a young man in good health as he approached his death, many things he did cannot be followed by terminally ill persons.)

6. How can memories tend our whole selves—body, heart, mind, and soul? Is there a particular memory—such as a favorite meal or other occasion or event—that tends your body, heart, mind, and soul? Why and how does this memory tend you? What specific religious celebrations, ceremonies, or sacraments tend each part of your being? Describe why this is so.

7. Look again at the descriptions of wholeness in this section. With Jesus as your model for tending toward wholeness, what is the next step for you to take on your own pilgrimage toward wholeness?